D0193854

HOW WE Worship

The Eucharist, the Sacraments, and the Hours

REV. LAWRENCE E. MICK

Liguori
LIGUORI, MISSOURI

Imprimi Potest:
Thomas D. Picton, C.Ss.R.
Provincial, Denver Province
The Redemptorists

Published by Liguori Publications
Liguori, Missouri
To order, call 800-325-9521
www.liguori.org

Library of Congress Cataloging-in-Publication Data

Mick, Lawrence E., 1946-
    How we worship : the Eucharist, the sacraments, and the hours / Lawrence E. Mick.
— 1st ed.
      p. cm.
   ISBN 978-0-7648-1936-0
   1. Catholic Church—Liturgy. I. Title.
   BX1970.M515 2009
   264'.02—dc22

                                                   2009043250

Liguori Publications, a nonprofit corporation, is an apostolate of the Redemptorists. To learn more about the Redemptorists, visit Redemptorists.com.

Printed in the United States of America
14 13 12 11 10   5 4 3 2 1
First edition

CONTENTS

PART FOUR: SENDING FORTH GOD'S PEOPLE

INTRODUCTION
The Meaning of Liturgy

The Gospel according to John begins with these words: "In the beginning was the Word." Our discussion of liturgy might also begin with the Word. What do we mean by the word "liturgy"? The dictionary defines liturgy as "a rite or body of rites prescribed for public worship." The *Catechism of the Catholic Church* says: "The word 'liturgy' originally meant a 'public work' or a 'service in the name of/on behalf of the people.' In Christian tradition it means the participation of the People of God in 'the work of God'" (1069).

Each definition gives us some important hints. The dictionary speaks of "rites," which we will consider shortly in more detail. Rites are patterns of behavior that enable a group of people to act together and to express matters of deep significance to them. The ritual nature of liturgy allows participants to engage in a common act of worship with some degree of ease because they know what comes next at any point.

The second definition in the dictionary for "liturgy" is "a eucharistic rite." Since the Eucharist is the central ritual of Christians, it is understandable that many people think that "liturgy" always means the Eucharist. In the Catholic tradition, however, liturgy includes all seven of the sacramental celebrations as well as the Liturgy of the Hours, sometimes called the Divine Office. These are the official acts of public worship carried out in the name of the whole Church.

Of course, there are many other ways that Christians pray, both individually and in groups. Every believer should pray on his or her own every day, and groups of believers gather for a variety of forms of prayer and devotion together. While these prayers, especially those shared in groups, have many aspects in common with liturgy, they are not included in the category of liturgy.

The catechism definition harkens back to the origin of the word in Greek. *Leitourgia* is commonly translated as "work of the people." It originally meant a public work, often done or paid for by a wealthy citizen on behalf of the community, such as providing a warship or building a gymnasium. Eventually, the meaning was extended to include any kind of public service, including public religious services.

In one sense, then, liturgy refers to work done on behalf of the people, but the catechism notes that in the Christian tradition it means the participation *of the people* as well. Liturgy is not something done by the priest or other ministers for a passive audience. It is the work of all gathered, who engage in the worship of God together.

Though different members of the community may carry out different roles within the liturgy, Christian worship is the responsibility and the activity of the whole assembly gathered together. Each member of the assembly has an essential role to play. In a sense, there is no audience at all. Some have suggested that the only audience at worship is God, to whom the worship is offered. But God also has a major role in the liturgy itself, as we shall see later.

THE LANGUAGE OF LITURGY

It is necessary for all those present who take part in the liturgy of the Church to have some basic knowledge of the language of worship. This is not primarily a matter of learning the meaning of a list of terms, but rather learning the ways that liturgy speaks, which includes much more than words. Liturgy is ritual action, and rituals are composed of symbolic objects, movements, and gestures along with spoken and sung words.

Some people find this necessity of learning liturgy's "vocabulary" a turn-off. They want to know why the liturgy can't be more readily accessible to a person who wanders in from the street.

This expectation is rather unrealistic, however. Any complex human activity has its own vocabulary and grammar. Think, for example, of the game of American football. Many people from other countries, where "football" is another name for soccer, find this American game quite confusing. This fact has led to various examples of humor, like the story of the young woman who accompanied her boyfriend to her very first football game. On the way out of the stadium, she told him she thought it was very silly for all those grown men to fight that long over twenty-five cents. When her boyfriend asked her what she was talking about, she noted that people were constantly shouting, "Get the quarter back!"

In 1953, a little-known comic named Andy Griffith gained national fame by describing a football game from the vantage point of a country boy at his first college game. The sketch was called "What It Was, Was Football," and he ended it with this description: "I think that it's some kindly of a contest where they see which bunchful of them men can take that punkin an' run from one end of that cow pasture to the other, without either gettin' knocked down or steppin' in somethin'!" So it seemed to one who didn't know the rules and vocabulary of the game.

Notice, too, that the vocabulary needed to understand a football game goes beyond spoken words. There are hand and arm gestures by the referees that tell much about what is happening on the field. Recognizing different formations and plays by the team requires some familiarity with the game and typical strategies. Even the cheerleaders have a repertoire of athletic moves that shape the overall experience of the crowd. And if you want to be a full participant in the event, you need to know how to act when various things happen during the game, whether it's just cheering when your team makes a good play or taking part in the "wave."

We find many similar realities when we examine the liturgy. While most anyone can sit on the sidelines and draw some benefit from the experience, those who want to really enter into the liturgy and draw the most from it need to learn its vocabulary and grammar. Some of this is purely verbal. There are words that are used in Christian worship that are not used in everyday speech, like *epiclesis* (invoking the Spirit) and *anamnesis* (the kind of remembering that makes the event present). Others are borrowed from everyday language but have different nuances, like "communion" and "consecration" and "remembrance."

The vocabulary of liturgy also goes beyond words. Meaning is conveyed, often more powerfully than words can manage, through symbols and ritual actions. These, too, must be learned and appreciated if a person wants to fully engage in the liturgical experience.

Symbols are often misunderstood in our society. A symbol is not the same as a sign. While a sign communicates some information, it generally refers us to something separated from itself. A billboard advertising a car dealer points us to the dealer's location, but you can't buy a car at the billboard. A symbol, on the other hand, somehow contains the reality it signifies. Consider a wedding ring after the death of a spouse, for example. That ring says far more than "I was married." It reminds the surviving spouse of a multitude of experiences and feelings from a life lived together. Or think of a kiss between lovers. The love is not somewhere else but somehow is contained in the kiss itself. Though the kiss does not contain all of the love, it does contain the reality it signifies. So, to say that a sacrament is a symbol is not to suggest it is not real. The sacramental symbol contains what it signifies.

Symbols are important in worship because they allow us to communicate realities that seem impossible to adequately express in words. They touch us on many levels at once, affecting our minds and hearts and spirits. Symbols may be strung together to form ritual actions, but even a single symbol is often an action rather than an object. It is what we do with water or oil or bread or wine that communicates the deep meaning we share in worship.

A FOUR-PART STRUCTURE

It is also important to understand the relationship between different parts of the liturgy. Though the liturgy has some unique vocabulary, it also draws on basic human activities to create its symbols and ritual patterns. Most liturgies follow the same basic structure as many other human gatherings.

This structure has four parts. The first is simply the gathering itself. People come together, whether for worship or for a party or for Thanksgiving dinner. The gathering involves more than just arriving at the same place. People greet one another, exchange pleasantries, and reconnect their lives.

Then there is a time for verbal sharing. At a party, this may be informal "catching up" on each other's lives.

At a testimonial dinner, it might be a speech about the one being honored. At Christian liturgy, it is a proclamation of the Word of God.

Most gatherings of people also involve some sharing of food and drink. This may be formal, like Thanksgiving dinner, or informal drinks and snacks when friends drop by. At the eucharistic liturgy, this corresponds to the sharing of consecrated bread and wine in Communion.

As common as it is to share food and drink when we gather, however, sometimes this central activity is different. People may gather for a concert or a work project that does not entail eating and drinking. So, too, Christians sometimes gather for worship that is centered around baptizing or anointing or reconciling. These activities then replace the meal as the central event.

Finally, as the gathering ends, people disperse. The game is over, the party comes to an end, the meal is finished, and people take leave of one another. In worship, we call this the dismissal.

These four parts of any human gathering will provide a framework for our discussion of the liturgy. We will focus most often on the liturgy of the Eucharist, since that is the central and most common liturgy the Church celebrates, but it will be easy to see how the celebration of the other sacraments fits the same general pattern.

The Liturgy of the Hours or Divine Office is a bit different than the sacramental liturgies, however. It also has a gathering and dismissal and includes a sharing of the

Word of God. But it does not have a clear central ritual element as the sacramental celebrations do. Its focus is on praise and thanksgiving, drawing on the psalms and biblical canticles and including prayers of intercession. It marks the times of the day and the cycles of seasons and feasts in the Church calendar. The *Catechism of the Catholic Church* says that the Liturgy of the Hours is "like an extension of the Eucharistic celebration" that makes the whole day holy by the praise of God (1174, 1178).

This, of course, is a goal of all liturgical celebrations. They are not celebrated for their own sake, but to sanctify our lives and our world. The liturgy seeks to bring us into contact with the presence and power of God, hoping that the experience will transform us so that we will be enabled to transform the world. What happens in Vegas may stay in Vegas, but what happens in the liturgy is meant to reach far beyond the time and place in which we celebrate.

Author's Note: As of this printing, a new missal is forthcoming that will include changes in the words we use in celebrating the Mass. It has been approved by the United States Conference of Catholic Bishops and is awaiting the Vatican's formal approval. Mass-related liturgical texts that are quoted in this book, therefore, first list the current wording in liturgy; then in parentheses is listed the wording of the upcoming missal.

JOE'S JOURNEY

Joe is a catechumen who has come to St. John's Parish to explore the possibility of becoming a Christian. After several months of inquiry, he made the decision to become a member of the Church. Having celebrated the rite of acceptance into the order of catechumens, he is recognized as part of the Church community, though he is still in formation. He is preparing for baptism, confirmation and the Eucharist, which he will receive at the Easter Vigil.

As a catechumen, Joe has been learning about the Bible, about the life and teaching of Jesus, about the history of the Church and about the way the Church prays and worships. He has been a bit surprised at how much there is to learn. When he first approached the parish to inquire about becoming Catholic, he thought it would be a short process. Now that he has become aware of how much he has to learn, he is grateful for the length of the catechumenate process. It is allowing him time to grow into a new way of life and to ask the many questions that he has about what the Church believes and how it lives out its faith.

Most of the gatherings of the catechumens include some form of prayer, often using things like candles, water, oil, and other items used in the Church's worship. This has allowed Joe to become comfortable with the way symbols can communicate the presence and action of God. He has also been learning the common responses that Catholics often use in the liturgy. He comes to Mass every Sunday, often accompanied by his sponsor, though he is dismissed along with the other catechumens after the Liturgy of the Word. He has begun to feel at home, here, as the rituals of the first part of the Mass and the prayer responses and hymns have become familiar to him.

MARY'S JOURNEY

Mary is a longtime member of St. John's. She was baptized as an infant and has been a member of this parish for the fifty years since she was married and moved to the area as a newlywed. Her children are grown and live in other cities. Her husband, Paul, died a couple of years ago. She now lives alone in the house she shared for so many years with her husband and children.

Mary, of course, has been comfortable at Mass for a long time. She has been worshipping in the Church for decades, so most of what happens seems almost automatic to her; she knows all the prayers and responses by heart. In recent years, though, she has come to realize that there is more to the liturgy than she had grasped in her earlier years. She's had more free time since her children left home and especially since Paul's death. She has come to a number of adult formation evenings at the parish, some of which have focused on the Mass and the sacraments. As a result, she is finding new depth in the liturgy. She has been paying more attention to the richness of the symbols that the community uses to express its faith and its worship of God. It's like a whole new way of understanding her faith has been opened up to her, and she is grateful for the spiritual gifts it has brought her.

RESOURCES FOR FURTHER READING

Cooke, Bernard J., and Gary Macy. *Christian Symbol and Ritual*. New York: Oxford University Press, 2005.

Kavanagh, Aidan. *Elements of rite: A Handbook of Liturgical Style*. Collegeville, MN: The Liturgical Press, 1990.

Mitchell, Leonel L. *The Meaning of Ritual*. New York: Paulist Press, 1977.

Turner, Paul. *Guide to the General Instruction of the Roman Missal*. Chicago: Liturgy Training Publications, 2003.

———. *Let Us Pray: A Guide to the Rubrics of Sunday Mass*. Collegeville, MN: Liturgical Press, 2006.

———. *ML Bulletin Inserts 3*. San Jose, CA: Resource Publications, 2007.

PART ONE

Gathering God's People

CHAPTER 1
Some Assembly Required

The first thing necessary for any liturgy is the assembly of the faithful. Liturgy is, by its very nature, a communal activity, so it requires people to come together with the intention of worshipping together.

This is not as simple as it first may seem, especially in our contemporary culture. We live in a consumer society and one that places a high value on individual preferences and decisions. These two aspects of our culture make it difficult for us to enter into a communal activity like liturgy.

Consumerism has become so thoroughly ingrained in our mentality that we may not even realize it. The influence of advertising in all our media, especially on television, constantly teaches us that shopping and buying things is the key to happiness and success in life. We are shaped by these messages even if we disagree with their assumptions. In 1955, economist Victor Lebow wrote in the *Journal of Retailing*, "Our enormously productive economy demands that we make consumption a way of life, that we convert the buying and use of goods into rituals, that we seek our spiritual satisfaction, our ego satisfaction, in consumption....We need things consumed, burned up, replaced, and discarded at an ever-increasing rate." This sounds almost like a description of a religion. Consumerism implies a way of life, has its own rituals, and offers the hope of spiritual satisfaction in consumption. The fact that this "religion" never really fulfills its promises has not kept it from dominating the lives of many people in our culture.

Another approach might give us some perspective. Since 1972, the kingdom of Bhutan in south Asia has tried to evaluate its national success by measuring its "gross national happiness," rather than the usual gross national product. This approach suggests that happiness requires spiritual development as well as material development. If that idea seems odd, it may simply indicate how thoroughly we have accepted the advertisers' message.

Consumerism has come to so dominate our thinking and our approach to life that we naturally tend to approach liturgy with the same mindset. Just as we go down the grocery aisle and pick out the cereal we prefer from among dozens of choices, we tend to approach worship with the expectation that we can take what we want from it and leave the rest. And if we don't find what we want in one place, we just take our business to another store or church. Moreover, we tend to approach liturgy as a product we consume rather than as an activity that we help to create. Many people think of the liturgy as something provided by the priest and the other liturgical ministers, and they then decide if they want to "buy" it or not.

Linked to this consumer mentality is our sense of individual rights and preferences. Our culture, perhaps more than any other in history, has exalted the individual above the community or society. While this certainly has many beneficial results in our respect for the rights of the individual, there are also negative effects when it becomes too dominant. The American mythos exalts the Lone Ranger, the self-made man or woman, the ones who pull themselves up by their own bootstraps, etc. We are less aware of the vital importance of the community in making and keeping us human and happy. As a result, many people find it difficult to relinquish their individual preferences for the sake of being part of and acting as a community.

Of course, most people learn the necessity of such self-denial when they enter into marriage and start a family. If the marriage is to last, both partners must learn to put the family ahead of personal desires. And they learn, perhaps to their surprise, that what seems like depriving themselves really leads to deeper happiness.

In a similar way, when we come to worship, we have to remember that liturgy is a communal activity. To take part in it often requires setting aside our individual likes and dislikes, our wishes and desires. Any communal activity requires such subsuming of the self into the group, whether it is a sports team trying for victory or a group of farmers at a barn raising. Can you imagine the shape of the barn if every person in the group insisted on doing it his or her own way? In worship, too, we are invited to be part of one communal act, which means none of us really gets to have our own way with it.

Sometimes people come to the liturgy expecting it to be their weekly time for private prayer. Because our lives are often so busy, many don't take time for private prayer during the week. They arrive at church hungry for quiet time to nourish their personal prayer life. They may then experience the sounds and activity of the liturgy as an intrusion, interrupting their prayer and frustrating their desire for peace and quiet.

There is no doubt that all of us need time for private prayer. It should be an integral part of every Christian's life, ideally on a daily basis. But the liturgy is communal prayer, and it is not intended to provide all of our prayer time for the week. When we come to the liturgy, we are gathering for communal prayer, which is a different kind of experience than our private prayer. We need both, each in its proper time and place.

To say that the liturgy is communal prayer, however, is not to say that it is not personal prayer. There is a big difference between personal and private. In the liturgy, we need to make the communal prayer intensely personal by entering into it fully. The liturgy prescribes various brief periods of silence to help us interiorize what is being said or sung or done, but we also need to be attentive throughout the ritual and make each part of it our own, not by changing it to suit us, but by embracing what the liturgy is expressing and letting it shape our attitudes to become more like those of Christ himself. It's a bit like being a musician in a band or a symphony orchestra. Each member of the group brings his or her uniqueness to the group effort, but each must play his or her part in tune with the piece of music being played. This certainly doesn't mean that any instrumentalist is not personally involved in the music, but it does require them to recognize that they are involved in a communal effort to produce a great sound. Similarly, in the liturgy, each person brings his or her personal relationship with God and with the community of faith and melds it into one great act of worship to praise God as the gathered assembly of God's holy people.

Another way to say this is that the assembly needs to reconstitute itself as an assembly. The individuals who gather need to reconnect to become a united assembly capable of the communal action of worship. This does not mean that individuals cease to have their own identity, of course. An assembly is made up of individuals who have agreed to become part of something larger than themselves.

JOE'S JOURNEY

Before Joe decided to join the catechumenate process at St. John's, he did a lot of "church shopping," looking for a church where he felt at home. He was hunting for a church that seemed to meet his needs and fit his tastes in worship. As he has gotten to know the community at St. John's, though, his approach has gradually shifted. Now he is trying to be open to what God is asking of him, and that includes letting go of some of his own preferences when he comes to church on Sunday. He is learning that to be part of the community's worship means becoming part of something larger than himself and his needs and tastes. One of the things he has come to value is his sense of belonging to this community that gathers for worship. He feels connected to others in the parish and, even though he only stays for part of the Mass, he feels like a part of this assembly as it praises God and listens to God's Word together. The leaders of the catechumenate have encouraged all the catechumens to develop a habit of daily prayer, and Joe has found this a powerful part of his spiritual growth. When he gathers with the parish community on Sunday, he brings the fruits of his private prayer into the liturgy.

MARY'S JOURNEY

When Mary comes to church each Sunday, she looks forward to seeing and chatting with friends she has known for many years. She has noticed that this has become much more important to her since Paul died. Even though she leads a fairly active life, she finds that living alone means that she spends much of the week by herself. When the weather is bad, she may go for several days without even seeing another person. So when she comes to church, she welcomes the sense of community that marks St. John's. It's quite a bit different than the parish in which she grew up. There, at least as well as she can recall it, people seemed to ignore one another in church. Everyone concentrated on their private prayers and focused their attention on the tabernacle where the Body of Christ was reserved. While that seemed proper at the time, she is glad that the people who gather at St. John's make an effort to connect with each other before the worship begins. It gives her a deep sense of belonging and being cared for, and she recognizes that as a gift of God's love in her life.

QUESTIONS FOR REFLECTION AND DISCUSSION

1. *How much do you think consumerism has influenced our culture? In what ways has it influenced your own values and behavior? Do you see the influence of consumerism on worship in your community?*

2. *Can you discern ways that our culture's emphasis on the individual has shaped your thinking? What are the positive effects? What are the negative implications?*

3. *Do you recognize liturgy as a communal activity? What implications does its communal nature have on the way you approach it and what you expect from it?*

4. *Do you think you have a good balance in your life between private prayer and communal prayer? Do you need to give more attention to one or the other? In what ways do they support each other?*

5. *Is there a real sense of "assembly" when your worship community gathers? What could you do to enhance that process?*

RESOURCES FOR FURTHER READING

Koesters, Anne. *Sunday Mass: Our Role and Why It Matters*. Collegeville, MN: The Liturgical Press, 2007.

Mick, Lawrence E. *Forming the Assembly to Celebrate the Mass*. Chicago: Liturgy Training Publications, 2002.

———. *Forming the Assembly to Celebrate the Sacraments*. Chicago: Liturgy Training Publications, 2002.

Mustafa, Nadia. "What About Gross National Happiness?" *Time,* Jan. 10, 2005: http://www.time.com/time/health/article/0,8599,1016266,00.html.

Revkin, Andrew C. "A New Measure of Well-Being From a Happy Little Kingdom," *New York Times*, October 4, 2005: http://www.gpiatlantic.org/conference/media/nyt1004.pdf.

We Gather in Christ: Our Identity as Assembly. Worship Office of the Archdiocese of Cincinnati. Chicago: Liturgy Training Publications, 1996.

CHAPTER 2
Remembering Who We Are

When we arrive at the door of the church, we need to remember who we are and why we are gathering. Often we do this quite naturally when we arrive at a gathering. If it is a party, we think of ourselves as party-goers. If it is a dance, we come prepared to be dancers (or wallflowers). If it is Thanksgiving dinner, we know our relationship to the others who are coming, and we come with big appetites. If it is a ball game, we come as fans or as players.

So who are we when we come to liturgy? A common error is to think of ourselves as an audience. The pews in most churches might suggest such an identity. We all sit in the "audience" section waiting for the actors up front to perform for us. If we like the performance, we will "pay for it" in the collection and come back for other productions in coming weeks. If we dislike it, we will go elsewhere or give up on church altogether.

In the liturgy, though, there is no audience. All of us are actors, charged with the responsibility of carrying out the liturgy. Good liturgy certainly requires competent presiders and preachers and musicians, but it also depends on the contributions of each member of the assembly, each doing his or her best to make the worship a full and rich experience of God's presence.

Those who have experienced Christian worship are aware of the vital roles of the presider, the musicians, the proclaimers of the Word, the preacher, and other ministers who serve in special roles during the liturgy. While each of these is important, it is crucial to understand that it is the assembly itself that is the primary minister of the liturgy. All those who serve in special roles do so in order to enable the assembly to carry out its role. It is the *whole* assembly, which of course includes the special ministers, who offers the communal act of praise to God.

The Christian tradition goes even farther. Through baptism, each of us becomes a member of the body of Christ. Though we retain our own identity, we are also part of Christ, making him present in the world today. When we gather for worship, we gather precisely as members of that body. We come together to make the body of Christ visible and to act together as that body in union with Christ, our head.

The worship we offer to God, then, is none other than the worship of Christ himself. We unite ourselves with his worship, with the praise he offers to the Father, with the sacrifice by which he redeemed the world. We can only properly carry out our responsibility at the liturgy as members of the body. Only insofar as we unite ourselves to Christ can we offer fitting worship and praise.

When we come to the liturgy, we also come as citizens of two realms. We live in our contemporary world and society, but we are also citizens of the kingdom of God. We come to the liturgy to connect our two realms. At the liturgy, we try to experience more fully what it means to live in the kingdom of God. We reaffirm our identity as members of the body of Christ. We recommit ourselves to living by gospel values. We treat one another as brothers and sisters, and we share signs of peace. We enter into intimate communion with one another, abandoning our striving for power and status. Here we are all equal before God. Here we are all gifted. Here we are all blessed. Here we are all special in God's eyes.

Then, when we leave the worship assembly, we try to carry with us a heightened awareness of who we are and who we are called to become. We try to bring a bit more of God's love and peace into our world. We carry on the mission of Christ that has been entrusted to us.

This is another aspect of our identity when we come to worship. We are those whom God has called to carry on the mission of Christ. Celebrating the liturgy fully requires some level of commitment to the worshipping community and to the work that it carries on. Though a casual visitor may find much of value in Christian worship—hearing God's word proclaimed, sharing in uplifting music, etc.—the full meaning and power of the liturgy will only be experienced by those who know that their lives are not their own, that they have been chosen by God to do God's work, and that they have been called to membership in this community to support that divine mission.

Even if we come with such a commitment, the liturgy will not disclose its full meaning to us the first time we come or the hundredth time. The liturgy is a rich and complex reality that we gradually come to appreciate more fully if we open ourselves to its dynamics and allow ourselves to be caught up in its mystery.

This dual citizenship we carry is another reason that it may take a bit of effort to enter into the liturgy. The words and symbols we use at worship are not always the same words and symbols we use in daily life. These two realms are interrelated but they are not the same. When we enter into worship we seek to enter more deeply into the true meaning of life and the mystery of existence. This requires language and expressions that go beyond our normal daily lives. Contemporary liturgical reform seeks to find a balance between immediately accessible language and the special words and symbols that can carry the weight of profound mysteries.

THE ENTRANCE RITES

The entrance rites of the liturgy are intended to remind us of who we are and what we are about to do. These rites vary in the different liturgies (baptism, Eucharist, etc.), but we can use the pattern of the Eucharist as a basic example.

We begin with an opening song. This song often expresses the focus of the particular celebration, such as a Christmas carol during the Christmas season or a song of sorrow during Lent. It serves to mark the formal beginning of the worship, and it also calls us into the communal action as we all join in singing the same words together.

Then we make the sign of the cross, reminding ourselves that we gather in the name of the Trinity and under the symbol of the cross. A simple greeting begins the dialogue between the presider and the assembly that will continue throughout the liturgy.

At most Eucharists, we have a brief penitential rite that can easily be misunderstood. It is not primarily a time to focus on our sins. It is a reminder that we are sinners, but even more importantly, it reminds us that our God is merciful. We can come into God's presence to share in worship because God has forgiven us. The penitential rite thus is not a reason to feel bad about ourselves, but a reason to be grateful to God.

On Sundays and feasts, we sing the *Gloria* (Glory to God), a hymn of praise. Though this once served as the opening song for the liturgy, it now stands as an opportunity to engage in pure praise of God for God's goodness and glory.

An opening prayer brings the entrance rites to a close. This prayer is called a "collect" because it is intended to *collect* the prayers of all those gathered in a generic spoken prayer. Thus the presider says, "Let us pray," inviting all to enter into a time of silence before the prayer is spoken.

The goal of these brief rites, according to the *General Instruction of the Roman Missal*, is "to ensure that the faithful who come together as one establish communion and dispose themselves to listen properly to God's word and to celebrate the Eucharist worthily" (46). Of course, they cannot accomplish these goals unless the worshippers come to the gathering aware of who they are and what they are assembling to do together.

JOE'S JOURNEY

When Joe first started coming to Mass at St. John's, he was very attentive to the preaching of the pastor and the quality of the music. He recognized and appreciated the effort being made by the preacher and the musicians to provide high-quality worship. The preaching was especially important to him and the other catechumens, because when they were dismissed after the homily, they continued to reflect on the Word of God and discussed how it might apply to their lives. A good homily was a great help to their discussions. When he first started coming, Joe found it difficult to participate very actively in the music and responses, but it wasn't long before he began to embrace his part in making the singing and the prayers of the liturgy his own. He recognizes that his participation helps make the worship more beautiful, and he tries to support others by his own efforts to sing and respond wholeheartedly.

MARY'S JOURNEY

Even though she had been coming to Mass for many years, Mary had to learn some of the same lessons as Joe did. After the Second Vatican Council in the 1960s, the pastor of St. John's urged all the people to enter more fully into the words and actions of the liturgy. They had gradually come to recognize that their efforts were a vital part of the worship. Even though it had been Church teaching for a long time, Mary found it hard to understand at first what it meant to say that everyone at Mass was part of the Body of Christ. It took her a while to make that insight her own, but now she looks forward to joining with all the other members of the Body to offer praise to God in union with Christ, their head. She values the unity she experiences with other members of the Body and the support they offer one another in their shared faith.

QUESTIONS FOR REFLECTION AND DISCUSSION

1. *What are your expectations when you come to the liturgy? What do you hope to gain from the experience? What are you willing to give?*

2. *Was the idea of the assembly as the primary minister of worship a new concept for you? Do you think your regular worship assembly is aware of its role?*

3. *Do you often think of yourself as a member of the Body of Christ? Have you been aware that we are invited to become part of Christ's act of worship in the liturgy? How might that thought affect your approach to worship?*

4. *How would you describe life in the kingdom of God? Do you get a sense of that in worship?*

5. *Are you aware at every liturgy that you are sent forth to carry on the mission of Christ? In what ways do you foster that mission? How does the liturgy help you to do so?*

6. *Contemporary liturgical reform seeks to find a balance between immediately accessible language and the special words and symbols that can carry the weight of profound mysteries. Do you think your experience of the liturgy reflects that balance? If not, which side needs more attention?*

7. *What parts of the entrance rite at Mass do you find most helpful in remembering who you are and why you are there?*

RESOURCES FOR FURTHER READING

Challancin, James. *The Assembly Celebrates: Gathering the Community for Worship*. New York/Mahwah: Paulist Press, 1989.

Ferrell, Karie, and Paul Turner. *Guide for Ushers and Greeters*. Chicago: Liturgy Training Publications, 2008.

Mick, Lawrence E. *Worshiping Well: A Mass Guide for Planners and Participants*. Collegeville, MN: The Liturgical Press, 1995.

———. *Guide for Ushers and Greeters*. Chicago: Liturgy Training Publications, 1997.

Pope John Paul II. *Dies Domini (The Day of the Lord)*, 1998: http://www.vatican.va/holy_father/john_paul_ii/apost_letters/documents/hf_jp-ii_apl_05071998_dies-domini_en.html, esp. Chapter III.

Pope Pius XII. *Mystici Corporis Christi* (the Mystical Body of Christ), 1943: http://www.vatican.va/holy_father/pius_xii/encyclicals/documents/hf_p-xii_enc_29061943_mystici-corporis-christi_en.html.

Searle, Mark. *Called to Participate*. Collegeville, MN: The Liturgical Press, 2006.

CHAPTER 3

Historical and Contemporary, Universal and Local

One of the sources of tension in the area of liturgical reform is the need to find the right balance between the universal and traditional nature of the liturgy and adaptation to the local culture and situation of a given assembly. The liturgy of the Church is not the creation of any one assembly or any one nation or culture. It comes to us already established by past generations and influenced through the centuries by a variety of cultures and other forces.

To attempt a history of the development of liturgy from the beginning is far beyond the scope of this book. We would have to begin with prehistory, when primitive humans began creating symbols and trying to worship their gods. Jewish liturgical forms drew upon earlier symbols and rituals to develop worship forms in response to their experience of God, who revealed the divine presence to Abraham and Moses and other figures of Jewish history. The Jewish Passover, for example, combined ritual observances of the springtime sacrifice of a young lamb to ensure fertility for the flock and a feast of unleavened bread offering the first fruits of the barley harvest. These two ancient rituals were given new meaning in light of the Exodus from Egypt and became Israel's central feast commemorating that historical event.

In a similar way, Christians drew on various Jewish rituals in developing Christian liturgies, but they were also reinterpreted in light of their experience of Jesus, especially of his death and resurrection. The Gospels note the link between the Eucharist and the Passover supper, and the eucharistic prayer has roots in Jewish prayers of praise and thanksgiving. Christian baptism has links to Jewish rites and the baptism practiced by John the Baptist. Yet the Christian view of both of these primary sacraments is radically based on the death and resurrection of Jesus.

Though it is a human creation developed over centuries of human history, the liturgy is also a gift to us from God. It is God's activity among the Israelites and our Christian ancestors that gave rise to the liturgy as we know it today. Moreover, the liturgy offers us the opportunity to encounter the living God in our midst, something that is only possible through God's gracious gift.

Because it is the gift of God, the liturgy is not our own possession to shape as we wish. It must remain faithful to the activity of God that it celebrates. It must also retain continuity with its historical roots, because ritual always has a traditional character. Though we can always probe more deeply into the meaning and purpose of any ritual, to some extent it is accurate to say that we do things a certain way "because that's the way we do it." Ritual is standardized behavior that draws much of its power from the fact that it is recognized as a time-honored mode of behavior. It links us to our history and inserts our personal lives into a broader sweep of human experience.

At the same time, ritual needs to be continually renewed. Traditional ways of acting sometimes need to be updated in light of changed circumstances. Though the liturgy is always linked to the past, it must also speak effectively to and for a given congregation at their moment in history. Thus good ritual is a blend of the traditional and the contemporary. It links current circumstances to the community's past and thus points the way toward the future.

The movement for liturgical reform, which reached a high point in the Catholic Church with the Second Vatican Council (1962–65) and has also involved most other Christian churches, seeks that balance between respect for the tradition and adaptation to contemporary needs. Most of the reforms implemented since the council are based on practices in earlier centuries, some of which were lost over time and have been recovered as a result of historical research. Drawing on the full scope of liturgical history rather than just recent centuries gives us a broader range of strategies and ritual elements for our worship today.

This reform effort, however, is not just historical reconstruction. The challenge is to draw from our past what can be useful again today, perhaps because the contemporary situation of the church is closer in some ways to its early history than to its more recent past. Consider the catechumenate as an example. This process of formation of adults for the sacraments of initiation (baptism, confirmation, and Eucharist) developed in the early church when the Christian community was a minority group in the culture and did not see its values widely reflected in the surrounding society. In succeeding centuries, in the age of Christendom, the church and society were more deeply linked, so that church leaders were often civic leaders and church values were at least professed by the society at large. In that era, at least in Europe, baptism was almost exclusively celebrated with infants, since few adults were not already baptized.

In recent times, the church has lost that broad control of the social atmosphere. Today we are again a minority in the culture, and we have adults coming to us to learn about Jesus and to join the Church. Thus the catechumenate has been reestablished as the way for adults today to prepare for initiation in the midst of the community of faith. It is an example of the Church fulfilling the words of Jesus: "Therefore every scribe who has been trained for the kingdom of heaven is like the master of a household who brings out of his treasure what is new and what is old" (Matthew 13:52).

Of course, sometimes the Church can get stuck in

retaining tradition for its own sake. There are many who feel that some of the most recent changes in the Church's liturgy are seeking to restore an approach that sees the past as always superior to anything new. It is a constant struggle to find the right balance, to preserve the tradition, but also to let it live and grow.

LOCAL AND CATHOLIC

One of the fundamental principles of the reform mandated by Vatican II is that the liturgy cannot be uniform throughout the world if it is to be the living prayer of the Church today. Each culture and language group brings to worship its own background and customs and style. In fact, each individual congregation also has its own unique elements and approaches, because each congregation is trying to live the Gospel at a particular place and time that is unique.

Thus the renewed liturgy offers a variety of ways that the standard ritual pattern can be adapted to local needs. There are multiple options for many of the prayers and other texts of the liturgy, for example, to be chosen according to local circumstances. Different styles of music on various instruments can reflect local traditions and cultures. The general intercessions (Prayer of the Faithful) are meant to be composed for each Mass by those on the local scene so that they reflect the needs of the day and the place where the liturgy is celebrated.

This local community, however, is also part of a universal (the meaning of the word "catholic") Church. We do not worship in isolation but in union with the whole Church throughout the world. Just as the standard ritual links us with generations who have gone before it, it also links us with assemblies of our brothers and sisters around the world. This means that there must be a balance between our local adaptation and our adherence to the basic pattern of worship established by the larger Church. Just exactly where that balance is found continues to be a debated question, but the liturgy needs to be both local and universal.

The universal character of the Church and of its liturgy has various implications. There are elements in the liturgy itself that express the links between the local community and the broader Church. In the eucharistic prayer, for example, we always pray for the pope and for the local diocesan bishop. This reminds us that we are part of a larger Church. In fact, historically, leaving out the name of the pope was a clear sign of schism from Rome.

Our prayer texts often pray for believers around the world, and today many parishes are learning to sing songs that come from various cultural traditions. This is especially important, of course, if the local parish is made up of several ethnic groups, but it is also appropriate for any assembly that recognizes its bonds to the universal Church.

This universal aspect of our worship also determines what feasts we celebrate and what texts of Scripture we use on a given day. While there are some variations in these, reflecting local adaptations to the universal calendar, the official liturgical books are very similar throughout the world.

Some experts argue that there should be more flexibility in the way that the liturgy is celebrated in different cultures. Vatican II called for such adaptation in the Constitution on the Sacred Liturgy. The *General Instruction of the Roman Missal* reaffirms that principle (*GIRM* 26). The basis for such cultural variations is ultimately theological. The Son of God took on the human condition in the Incarnation. This means that God is to be found in the human and the created. So the liturgy needs to be firmly planted in the local soil. It should not be something foreign to those who gather for worship. Whatever local adaptations are made, however, will still need to be balanced with the fact that local worshippers are part of a larger Church.

JOE'S JOURNEY

When Joe first started coming to St. John's, he was surprised to find that Catholic worship didn't seem all that different from many of the other churches he had visited. He had heard comments from people for many years about how strange the Catholic Mass was, but he was pleased to discover that it was not all that difficult to understand and follow. In the catechumenate sessions, they had discussed the changes that had occurred in the Catholic liturgy in the 1960s, and he found it hard to imagine trying to worship in Latin. He was glad that things had changed before he started exploring the Catholic Church. He values many of the traditional elements of the Catholic Mass, but he's glad that it is conducted in English today. He knows that the liturgy would sound much different if he traveled to another country, since it would be celebrated in the local language there. Yet he also recognizes that it would still be the same Mass, the same liturgy at its heart. Even when he travels to a different part of the country and finds a Catholic church there, he finds differences in style and tone, but it is easy to recognize the liturgy as fundamentally the same as what he experiences at home.

Mary's Journey

When Mary thinks about how her approach to worship has changed over her lifetime, she is a bit amazed. At one time in her life, she was certain that the Church would never change. Then Pope John XXIII called the Second Vatican Council, and all sorts of things changed in the Church. The most obvious changes to many people were in the way the Church worshipped. After years of worshipping mostly in silence and saying the rosary or other prayers during Mass, the Church encouraged everyone to take a more active part in the liturgy. The congregation gradually learned a large number of new hymns and learned all the spoken parts of the Mass by heart. They had some good laughs at times, sometimes a bit embarrassed by their difficulties carrying a tune or their stumbling through the texts of the longer prayers. But over time, they came to embrace their role at Mass, and now it seems that it was always that way.

There was a time when Mary complained about the fact that liturgy was different from one parish to the next. When she was young, she often heard that you could go to Mass anywhere in the world and it would be the same. After the changes, she knew that Mass would seem very different in Mexico than in the United States. In fact, she found on vacation that it was very different in New Mexico, too. While she admitted that this made sense, she still regretted that the liturgy wasn't the same all over the world. Recently, Mary had an opportunity to attend a Mass said in Latin, according to the rite in force before the council. She had looked forward to it, remembering how much the Mass had meant to her as a child. But she was surprised to discover that it seemed so strange to her now, and that she missed being able to lift her own voice to praise God in song and prayer. It was then that she realized that the renewed liturgy had really taken root in her heart and her life.

QUESTIONS FOR REFLECTION AND DISCUSSION

1. *What elements of the liturgy in your experience speak of the traditional nature of ritual worship? How do such elements affect you? Are they comforting or do they seem outdated?*

2. *Do you recognize elements in Christian worship that have been adopted from earlier traditions? How many can you name?*

3. *In what ways is the liturgy you experience adapted to current times? How does such adaptation help or hinder your engagement in the worship? Do you think the twentieth century reforms of the liturgy show a good balance between the traditional and the contemporary?*

4. *What elements in your experience of worship speak to you of the universal character of the liturgy? Are you often aware of your links to Christians around the world as you worship? What fosters such awareness?*

5. *In what ways is the liturgy adapted to your local community and its needs? Are there ways you can see to adapt it more effectively?*

RESOURCES FOR FURTHER READING

Baldovin, John F. *Reforming the Liturgy: A Response to the Critics.* Collegeville, MN: The Liturgical Press, 2008.

Francis, Mark. *Shape a Circle Ever Wider: Liturgical Inculturation in the United States.* Chicago: Liturgy Training Publications, 2000.

Marini, Piero. *A Challenging Reform: Realizing the Vision of the Liturgical Renewal.* Collegeville, MN: The Liturgical Press, 2007.

White, James F. *Roman Catholic Worship: Trent to Today.* Collegeville, MN: The Liturgical Press, 2003.

CHAPTER 4
Church Music and Architecture

One of the more obvious manifestations of the local and universal character of the liturgy in our own time is the wide variety of music that is used in contemporary worship. Different liturgical celebrations can have very different styles of music and yet be part of the same liturgical tradition. Even within a given worship service, multiple types of music may blend in an aural tapestry, uniting traditional and contemporary sounds from several different cultural backgrounds.

There is an approach to worship that considers only certain types of music and certain instruments as acceptable in the liturgy. Often that means only organ music written in past centuries. For some people, this traditional style "sounds like church" and provides both comfort and a support for prayer.

A much older tradition, however, reminds us that various instruments and musical styles can be used to offer praise and thanks to God. In the Bible, Psalm 150 calls us to "Praise him with trumpet sound; praise him with lute and harp! Praise him with tambourine and dance; praise him with strings and pipe! Praise him with clanging cymbals; praise him with loud clashing cymbals!" Through the ages, people have used many different instruments and various musical styles to enliven their worship of God, and contemporary church documents affirm and encourage such diversity.

Music serves a number of functions in the liturgy. One of the most obvious is that it unifies the assembly's voice. Trying to recite texts together in a large group is very difficult, if not impossible. The rhythm of music enables even large assemblies to stay together, singing the same words at the same time on (at least generally) the same notes. This unifying function of music is very important for worship, for it helps us move from the individual mode of action to the communal mode necessary for the worship event.

Music also adds beauty to the liturgy. It lifts it beyond the realm of the ordinary to the arena of the beautiful and uplifting. Music gives voice to dimensions of meaning that go beyond what words alone can express. It also adds a measure of solemnity to the celebration and invites the worshippers to enter into the experience emotionally as well as intellectually. Music adds elements of joy and other emotions that mere words cannot provide.

Singing particular parts of the liturgy highlights those elements of the liturgy, emphasizing their importance. Every liturgical celebration has its own rhythm, with some elements being more central than others. Music, properly employed, can make clear which elements are more important by giving them a fuller and more powerful expression.

These benefits that music offers, of course, are dependent on the quality and appropriateness of the music. While the liturgy does not require concert-level professionals, it does need musicians with a basic competence and a commitment to practice and prepare well.

The appropriateness of a particular piece of music rests on several principles. One is that the music itself should be of good quality. That does not mean that it has to be a particular style of music. There is good gospel music as well as good Gregorian chant, good folk music as well as good polyphony. But the music must be a solid composition and be executed well if it is to serve the prayer of the community.

A second principle is that the music must fit the assembly that has gathered to celebrate. To be pastorally effective, it needs to engage those who have gathered. This does not mean that worshippers should not be stretched at times to become comfortable with other musical styles, but it does mean that musicians need to be attentive to the cultural backgrounds and musical sensibilities of each assembly.

The third and most important principle is that the music must be liturgically appropriate. Music in the liturgy does not stand on its own but must be an integral part of the act of worship. Music has a ministerial function. It must serve the needs and requirements of the liturgy itself. Its task is to assist the members of the assembly in expressing their faith and entering into the act of worship as fully as possible. The music chosen should fit the particular part of the liturgy, supporting its meaning and dynamics. It is not enough that the music be generically spiritual or popular with the people. It must harmonize with the liturgy itself and support the purpose of that particular part of the liturgy.

A couple of examples may help clarify this point. An acclamation, like the Alleluia and verse before the proclamation of the Gospel, needs to be musically strong and relatively brief. An extended polyphonic arrangement from the eighteenth century may be beautiful, but it will not function well as an acclamation of the assembly. The communion song is intended to accompany the communion procession and reflect the meaning of Communion. This is the high point of the community's union with Christ and with one another in Christ, so the song should foster that sense of unity. It also needs to be sung by people who are moving in procession, so it should be well known or a song with a refrain that people can remember without carrying hymnals. Because its function is to accompany the communion procession, it should begin when the procession starts and last until all have received.

This ministerial function of music in the liturgy can be a source of tension if musicians and choir members do not understand their role properly. Since it is the whole assembly that is the primary actor in the liturgy, all the special ministers, including the music ministry, are intended to help the assembly to fully carry out its role. That does not mean that a choir cannot occasionally do a motet or other choir piece, for example, but it means that their role is not to be performers seeking the acclaim of the assembly, but ministers helping the assembly to pray and worship well.

A HOUSE FOR THE CHURCH

Just as music must serve the needs of the liturgy, the building in which worship occurs must also serve those needs. This is the source of much confusion in modern times because the understanding of the liturgy has changed and thus the architectural requirements for the liturgy are different than they were when many current church buildings were erected.

In the recent past, many Catholic churches were really designed as shrines for the tabernacle. The tabernacle holding the reserved Eucharist was the visual focal point of the building, often surrounded by impressive art work, and the Mass was celebrated right in front of the tabernacle.

Many Protestant churches, on the other hand, were constructed and arranged to focus on the pulpit, since their worship revolved primarily around the proclamation and preaching of the Word of God.

Contemporary liturgical renewal in many Christian churches has led to rethinking the ideal shape and arrangement of worship spaces. Though we often speak of the building as "the church," it might more properly be called "the home of the church." The church is the assembly of God's people; the church building is where the church gathers for worship.

This focus on the assembly leads to principles for church architecture that are different from those of the recent past. The primary question is what activities the church will carry out in the space. Then the space is designed and arranged to facilitate those activities (see *GIRM* 294).

An architectural critic for a local paper once reviewed a church built shortly after Vatican II and complained that it looked like they had decided what they were going to put inside and then just put a skin over it. When the pastor read the review, he commented that this is exactly what they did! Though a church structure certainly can be an impressive building from the outside, it is what happens inside that should determine the design of the building.

Attention to the importance of the assembly has led many contemporary churches to be built so that members of the assembly can see each other during worship, rather than seeing only the backs of the heads of those in the pew in front of them. Some churches have abandoned pews altogether. While pews provide the maximum seating capacity for a given space, they tend to inhibit the movement of the assembly. Movable seating offers more flexibility when the worship space is used for different liturgies.

This functional approach to designing worship spaces also shapes decisions about the placement of the altar, the pulpit, the presider's chair, the baptismal font, and other focal points for prayer and worship. Embracing a functional approach does not mean, however, that there is no place for good art and beautiful surroundings. The worship space should help those gathered to lift up their minds and hearts to God, and good art and a beautiful environment can be a great help to this.

The style of the building and the art that is used in it should naturally reflect the style and sensibilities of the era in which it is built. There is a tendency to cling to former styles of architecture and art because they "look like church," but such nostalgia is not a good basis for artistic decisions. Older buildings may even need remodeling at times if they have become too dated or if they do not allow the full celebration of the current rites of the church. Just as we remodel our homes from time to time, the house of the church can also be updated to reflect current styles and needs (see *Built of Living Stones*, 48).

One major change in many Catholic churches is the provision of a baptismal font that allows for immersion of both infants and adults. Other changes have been made in many parishes to allow better accessibility for those with physical limitations. This includes not only enabling such people to get into the church itself but also allowing them access to the ambo and other places where ministers function. Many newer or renovated churches have also created a separate chapel for reservation of the Eucharist. This provides a quiet place for prayer and adoration while not encouraging the assembly to focus on the reserved sacrament during the celebration of the Eucharist itself.

JOE'S JOURNEY

One of the first challenges that confronted Joe when he started taking part in the Mass was the singing. He had never been much of a singer. Even at birthday parties, he tried to sing very softly so no one would hear him. He thought his singing voice was pretty awful, so when the catechumenate leaders taught the group that singing was an essential part of Catholic worship, he resisted the idea. It took him a while to accept the fact that he didn't have to be a great singer to take part in the worship. It helped when his sponsor told him that God had given him that voice, so it was okay to give it back to God in song!

As part of their catechumenate journey, the group had taken several trips to other churches, including the diocesan cathedral. Joe was struck by the fact that Catholic churches could look so different from one another. There were many different architectural styles and artistic expressions in these different places, but all of them, he noticed, had prominent places for the ambo (lectern from which the Scripture is proclaimed), the altar, and the presider's chair. They all had obviously been either designed or remodeled to fit the way the Church carries out its worship today.

MARY'S JOURNEY

Mary had always liked singing. She had taken part in musical productions in grade school and high school, and she had been a member of the glee club at college. Still, it was a strange idea to her at first when the pastor said that the whole assembly was supposed to sing the parts of the Mass as well as the hymns. She could easily see the role of the choir; they were trained, and they practiced every week to be able to sing well. But the assembly as a whole was much less polished. She wondered if God would not be more pleased with beautiful choir music. Over time, though, she came to see that it was the effort of each member of the assembly to praise God in song that mattered more than perfect harmony. Now when the assembly begins the Mass with the opening song, she senses the unity that singing expresses as the whole assembly (well, at least *most* of those present) joins their voices together to praise the Lord.

What Mary found even more difficult, though, were the changes that were made in the church building after the council. They took out the beautiful marble altar that faced the wall and put in a new altar facing the people. And they moved the statues of the saints from the front of the church to the back. It seemed almost a sacrilege to change things that people were so used to seeing when they came to church. It was only after she had visited a number of other Catholic churches, including ones built after the council, that she began to understand why these renovations were needed to support the renewed liturgy. Now she proudly shows her church to visitors and points out the beauty of the new altar and ambo. She also tells them that the statues of the saints that now stand behind and alongside the assembly remind them that they worship in the company of all the saints and angels.

QUESTIONS FOR REFLECTION AND DISCUSSION

1. *What type of music do you find most appropriate for worship? How open are you to other styles?*

2. *Do you experience music as a unifying force in worship? Does it help you unite yourself with the rest of the assembly? Are different musical preferences divisive, or can they be mutually enriching?*

3. *Singing should highlight the more important parts of the liturgy. Does that happen in your experience? Which parts of the liturgy are sung most often?*

4. *Could you explain to someone else what it means to say that music has a ministerial function?*

5. *What is your reaction to traditional church buildings and contemporary ones? How does the architecture of the building help or hinder your prayer and worship? What are the elements that affect you the most?*

6. *Does the architecture of your worship space really facilitate the role of the assembly? What could help the assembly to recognize and fulfill its central role?*

Resources for Further Reading

Built of Living Stones: Art, Architecture, and Worship. Washington, DC: National Conference of Catholic Bishops/United States Catholic Conference, 2000.

Boyer, Mark G. *The Liturgical Environment.* Collegeville, MN: The Liturgical Press, 2004.

Harmon, Kathleen. *The Ministry of Music: Singing the Paschal Mystery.* Collegeville, MN: The Liturgical Press, 2004.

Joncas, Jan Michael. *From Sacred Song to Ritual Music: Twentieth-Century Understandings of Roman Catholic Worship Music.* Collegeville, MN: The Liturgical Press, 1997.

Mauck, Marchita. *Shaping a House for the Church.* Chicago: Liturgy Training Publications, 1990.

———. *Places for Worship.* Collegeville, MN: The Liturgical Press, 1995.

Sing to the Lord: Music in Divine Worship. Washington, DC: United States Conference of Catholic Bishops, 2007.

Vosko, Richard S. *God's House Is Our House: Re-imagining the Environment for Worship.* Collegeville, MN: The Liturgical Press, 2006.

PART TWO

Encountering God's Word

CHAPTER 5
Hearing the Word of the Lord

I f we have entered into the entrance rites and allowed
them to remind us of our identity and our purpose,
then we are probably ready to hear the Word of the
Lord addressed to us in the readings and the homily.

When we speak of the Word of the Lord in this con-
text, we mean more than the fact that we proclaim the
written Word of God in the Scriptures. In the Christian
tradition, the proclamation of the Word in the midst of
the assembly is recognized as a current event in which
Christ speaks to his people gathered as his body. The
Constitution on the Sacred Liturgy puts it simply: "He
is present in his word since it is he himself who speaks
when the holy scriptures are read in church" (*SC* 7).

This understanding of the Liturgy of the Word moves
us beyond any idea that this is a time for studying the
Bible or learning Church doctrine. While both of those
are important, and some things may in fact be learned as
we hear the Word proclaimed, the purpose of this part
of the liturgy is not study but a spiritual encounter with
the living Christ.

The Liturgy of the Word is thus intended to be a spiritual event, an opportunity to encounter the Lord as he speaks to us. Here's how Pope John Paul II put it:

> It should also be borne in mind that *the liturgical proclamation of the word of God*, especially in the Eucharistic assembly, is not so much a time for meditation and catechesis as *a dialogue between God and his People*, a dialogue in which the wonders of salvation are proclaimed and the demands of the Covenant are continually restated. On their part, the People of God are drawn to respond to this dialogue of love by giving thanks and praise, also by demonstrating their fidelity to the task of continual "conversion."
>
> *DIES DOMINI* ("THE DAY OF THE LORD"), 41

If we recognize this as a moment of dialogue, then our response becomes obvious. When someone speaks to us, we should listen. This is not a time to be reading the text from a book, but a time to engage fully with the one speaking to us. Through the lector or deacon or priest, we hear Christ speak to us, so our eyes and our attention should be focused on the speaker. As the disciples gathered around Jesus to listen to him, hanging on every word, so we gather to hear him speak in our own time.

Hearing the Word proclaimed in the midst of the assembly is a communal experience. We certainly can and should read the Bible on our own as part of our personal spiritual discipline. But in the assembly we listen together, as members of the body of Christ being guided by Christ, our head. Within that communal experience, though, each person might hear the Word a bit differently. The Holy Spirit, who inspired the scriptural writings, also enables the listener to hear the message that Christ has for each person.

In one of the episodes of the newspaper comic "The Lockhorns," Leroy is looking at a Word-a-Day Calendar in a store window. He comments to a friend, "That would be an appropriate gift, since that's how often I get one in with Loretta." God may feel a lot like that with us. We tend to address words to God much more often than we listen. And God may only hope to get one word in. During the Liturgy of the Word, it is perhaps an unreasonable expectation of ourselves to hope to catch every word and grasp every idea. In the three readings, the psalm, the Gospel acclamation, and the homily, there are far too many words for any of us to fully comprehend everything. What is crucial is that we are listening attentively to the Word of the Lord that Christ wants each of us to hear. It may happen that we are struck by a word (or idea) in the first reading and, as a result, we don't even hear the rest of the reading or the next one. That's not necessarily a bad thing. If that word of the Lord has touched us and taken root in us, that may be enough for one week. It may be more than many people take home who have tried to "get it all."

The structure of the Liturgy of the Word is that of a dialogue. For Sundays and solemnities, we hear three readings. The first reading is generally drawn from the Hebrew Scripture (the Old Testament), though in the Easter Season, we hear from the Acts of the Apostles. Then we respond to God's Word with the responsorial psalm. This psalm is often sung in responsorial form, with a response sung by all and verses sung by a cantor or choir. It is called "responsorial" because it is a response to the first reading in some way, often echoing its message or complementing it. It provides us a way to reply to the Word we have heard.

The second reading is generally drawn from the letters of Saint Paul or one of the other letters of the New Testament or the Book of Revelation. This reading is followed by the Gospel acclamation, which accompanies the procession with the Book of Gospels. It acclaims Christ whose life and message we then proclaim from a passage drawn from one of the four Gospels. The lectionary is arranged in a three-year cycle, and we focus primarily on one of the synoptic Gospels (Matthew, Mark, and Luke) in each of those years, turning to the Gospel of John mostly during Lent and Easter each year.

The liturgy is also intended to have periods of silence at several points. In the Liturgy of the Word, silence is recommended before the first reading begins, after the first and second reading, and after the homily. The silences after the readings are intended to be significant enough in length to allow the listeners to reflect upon and embrace the word they have just heard. Here's how the *General Instruction of the Roman Missal* puts it:

The Liturgy of the Word is to be celebrated in such a way as to promote meditation, and so any sort of haste that hinders recollection must clearly be avoided. During the Liturgy of the Word, it is also appropriate to include brief periods of silence, accommodated to the gathered assembly, in which, at the prompting of the Holy Spirit, the word of God may be grasped by the heart and a response through prayer may be prepared.

GENERAL INSTRUCTION
OF THE ROMAN MISSAL, 56

JOE'S JOURNEY

When Joe arrived at church one Sunday, he was feeling pretty good. He had just gotten word from his boss that he would be getting a promotion soon, which would bring with it a nice raise. As he settled into his seat, he said a prayer of thanks to God for this blessing and for all the ways that God had blessed his life. When the lector began to proclaim the first reading, which came from the prophet Amos, he was struck by the intensity of the prophet's condemnation of the well-off: "Woe to the complacent in Zion!" In the silence after the reading, Joe began to wonder if those words applied to him. Later, when the priest proclaimed the Gospel reading about the rich man and Lazarus, the same question confronted Joe. He was beginning to understand how the Word of God can afflict the comfortable—not just comfort the afflicted.

MARY'S JOURNEY

When Mary came to church that same day, she was feeling a bit worried. Since her husband's death, she had been getting by on her social security check and some income from investments in a mutual fund. But the stock market had not been doing well lately, and she just received a notice that the cost for her supplemental health insurance was going up significantly. She wasn't sure how she was going to continue to make ends meet. So, when she heard the words of Amos and the Gospel parable of the rich man and Lazarus, she found the readings reassuring. They reminded her that God cared for the poor and the weak, the orphan and the widow, and that helped her to renew her trust in God's providence in her own life.

QUESTIONS FOR REFLECTION AND DISCUSSION

1. *How aware are you that it is Christ who speaks to you when the Scriptures are proclaimed in the midst of the assembly? What would help you to hear Christ's voice more clearly through the lector, deacon, or priest? What makes it difficult for you?*

2. *Can you recall when the Word of the Lord really struck home? What do you think made the Word more powerful? What effect did those experiences have on your life?*

3. *Do you find it difficult to listen attentively to the proclamation of the Word? What makes it difficult? What makes it easier?*

4. *Do you experience the Liturgy of the Word as a reflective, meditative time? What helps make it so for you, or what keeps it from being so?*

5. *Does your worshipping community allow significant periods of silence after the first two readings and after the homily? Are you able to enter into these silences fruitfully? What value do you see in such silences?*

RESOURCES FOR FURTHER READING

Bonneau, Normand. *The Sunday Lectionary: Ritual Word, Paschal Shape*. Collegeville, MN: The Liturgical Press, 1998.

Connell, Martin. *Guide to the Revised Lectionary*. Chicago: Liturgy Training Publications, 1998.

"Introduction to the Lectionary," *The Liturgy Documents: A Parish Resource*, 3rd Edition. Chicago: Liturgy Training Publications, 2000.

Janowiak, Paul. *The Holy Preaching: The Sacramentality of the Word in the Liturgical Assembly*. Collegeville, MN: The Liturgical Press, 2000.

Proclaim the Word: The Lectionary for Mass: Study Text VIII. The Bishops' Committee on the Liturgy. Washington, D.C.: USCC Publications Office, 1982.

Rosser, Aelred. *Guide for Lectors*. Chicago: Liturgy Training Publications, 1998.

The Bible Documents: A Parish Resource. Lysik, David, ed. Chicago: Liturgy Training Publications, 2001.

CHAPTER 6
Called to Conversion

The proclamation and hearing of God's Word is not intended as simply a casual conversation. When God speaks, that word is a word of power. This is the same word that created the universe from nothing. This is the word that prophets felt compelled to preach. This is the word of which Isaiah said: "For as the rain and the snow come down from heaven, and do not return there until they have watered the earth, making it bring forth and sprout, giving seed to the sower and bread to the eater, so shall my word be that goes out from my mouth; it shall not return to me empty, but it shall accomplish that which I purpose, and succeed in the thing for which I sent it" (55:10–11). This is the word that reached its fullness in Jesus, the Word Incarnate.

The proclamation of God's Word in our midst, therefore, is intended to have an effect on the hearers. As one wit put it, the word is intended to comfort the afflicted and afflict the comfortable. Christ often speaks a word of comfort, proclaiming God's love for every person, even the greatest sinner. The message of the Gospel is fundamentally a message of reconciliation, a message of forgiveness. Christ came to reconcile us to the Father and to one another. In his life and in his teaching, Jesus showed God's compassion toward the sick and the suffering, the outcast and the sinner, the prisoner and the oppressed. The Word of God is often a word of comfort.

But Christ also calls us to conversion. From the very beginning of his preaching ministry, he called people to "Repent and believe in the gospel" (Mark 1:15). To repent means to change one's life. Christ's preaching is a call to conversion of mind and heart. Sometimes the word we hear is a word of challenge, calling us to rethink the way we understand the world and the way we live our lives. Even when the word we hear is a word of consolation, it is an invitation to open our hearts to God's love, to accept God's mercy, to embrace God's wisdom.

Conversion is the ultimate goal of the Liturgy of the Word, because it is the goal of the liturgy as a whole. We can understand the purpose of liturgy in two directions. It certainly is intended to give praise and thanks to God. In one sense, it needs no other justification. God is God and we are not, and thus it is appropriate for us to praise God and to thank God for all that we have received.

At the same time, the liturgy is not just our prayer addressed to God. It is also God's action toward us. The liturgy is a primary place where we and God meet and interact, and that interaction always calls us to change. We cannot come into contact with the living God and come away unchanged.

The process of conversion is basic to the whole Christian life. Some traditions speak of conversion as the result of a significant moment when one accepts the Lord as one's Savior. The Catholic tradition, along with many others, recognizes the value of special moments of spiritual growth but sees conversion as a journey that really lasts a lifetime. For those baptized in infancy, their whole lives are a process of growing into their identity as children of God and members of the body of Christ. For those who come to faith at a later age, there is an initial conversion process that leads to the sacraments of initiation, but their conversion journey also continues. Every day we confront choices to follow the Lord or to turn away from Gospel values. Every day we are invited to deepen our relationship with the Lord, to grow in our love for him, to embrace more fully the will of the Father as he did.

Thus conversion is not just a process for those joining the Church ("converts," we often call them), but a journey for every believer throughout his or her life. Recognizing this call from God to a life of continual conversion is important for a proper understanding of the liturgy and how it is intended to shape our lives.

The liturgy can be understood as a school of conversion. The dynamics of the liturgy continually call us into deeper relationship with the Lord and with all the members of Christ's body. Responding to these dynamics is the primary way that we grow in the spiritual life. As the Constitution on the Sacred Liturgy puts it, participation in the liturgy "is the primary, indeed the indispensable source from which the faithful are to derive the true Christian spirit" (*SC* 14).

The liturgy draws us into the very life of the Trinity. We share in the *Father's* will for the salvation of the world, in *Christ's* redemptive death and resurrection, and in the *Holy Spirit's* love that is our bond of unity and the motive for our mission. This is what we mean when we say that the liturgy or the sacraments are a means of grace. Grace is not a commodity that we receive but a sharing in the life of God. The liturgy enables us to enter more fully into that life, a movement that can be described as an increase of grace. As we are drawn step by step more deeply into the life of God, we grow in holiness.

The Constitution also says that through the liturgy, "the work of our redemption takes place" (*SC* 2). Liturgy is not just something *we* do. It is also the work of *God* continuing in our time. We are invited to share in this work by uniting our wills with God's saving will, by entering into the mystery of the death and resurrection of Christ, and by embracing and allowing ourselves to be embraced by the love of the Holy Spirit. If salvation is ultimately a matter of God bringing the world into God's own life, God continues to bring that about through the liturgy, first by drawing us into the divine life and then by sending us out to draw others to Christ and ultimately into the life of the Trinity. When we celebrate the liturgy, we share in God's redeeming work. Making us and all the world holy is God's purpose, and the liturgy is a primary way that God accomplishes that growth in holiness.

The liturgy seeks to foster our spiritual growth by shaping our attitudes, because our behaviors flow from those attitudes. The liturgy presents us with values that are often different from the values of our culture. If we embrace those values, then our attitudes will be gradually reshaped to match those of Christ more than those of our society.

Some of those values are presented in words. As we listen to the proclamation of the readings, the preaching in the homily, the words of the intercessions, the language of the eucharistic prayer, and other texts in the liturgy, we are invited to make the values and ideas presented there our own.

Other values are communicated non-verbally in the symbols and rituals we employ in the liturgy. Sharing the sign of peace, for example, invites us into relationships with those around us based on our unity in Christ. Everyone sharing the same small amount of consecrated bread and wine at Communion speaks of our equality before God. Treating each other with respect and care at worship reminds us to do the same outside the church walls.

Of course, these values are only able to shape our attitudes if we embrace them. One certainly can attend worship services repeatedly and reject the values expressed there so that nothing changes in one's attitudes or behavior. One might ask such a person why they bother coming to worship, however. If we are not willing to change, what is the point? Do we not come to church each week in order to become better people? That requires change, which only happens if we cooperate with God's grace and allow God to reshape our attitudes and our behavior.

Many of the points we have highlighted earlier are also some of the ways that the liturgy invites us to change. To enter into the worship itself, we have to let go of our own preferences and become part of the communal action. That requires some self-denial and an openness to others around us. It may require opening our hearts when we would rather stay closed in our own safe space. Joining in the opening song requires us to go further out of ourselves, especially if we don't enjoy the particular song or if we think our voice is not that good. When we celebrate the penitential rite, we are invited to embrace humility, recognizing our sinfulness at the same time we embrace again the mercy of God offered to us. Listening to the Word proclaimed requires an attentive focus and open ears, but even more, it requires an open heart that is ready to accept what the Lord has to say to us.

All the way through the ritual, the liturgy calls us to embrace the meaning of the words and actions we share. If we do so regularly, the liturgy will reshape us, day by day, bit by bit, more and more into the image of Christ himself, whose worship we share.

JOE'S JOURNEY

Since he started coming to the catechumenate sessions, Joe had heard the word "conversion" many times. It was a constant theme in the catechists' teaching, and they led the group to reflect often on how God was at work in their lives, calling them to change their thinking and their behavior. He had come to understand that the conversion process of dying to selfishness and rising to a new way of life was the main goal of the catechumenate experience. And he also recognized that God's call to conversion was often heard through the Word of God proclaimed in the midst of the assembly at Mass. The catechumens' discussions breaking open the Word after they were dismissed from Mass often focused on what that Word demanded of them and how they might live it out in the week ahead. At first, this emphasis on conversion felt rather demanding, like God was asking an awful lot of him. Over time, though, he came to see that his efforts to change his ways were leading him to a happier and more satisfying life. He sees that he has a long way to go, but he is grateful now for the grace of conversion that God has given him.

MARY'S JOURNEY

Mary had heard the word "conversion" many times through the years, too, but for a long time she didn't think it had much to do with her. She thought of "converts" as those who joined the Church as adults, but *she* had been Catholic all her life. At a parish mission a few years ago, the mission speaker had asked how many in the assembly were converts. When only a few people raised their hands, he asked what was wrong with the rest of them! Then he proceeded to explain that conversion was a lifelong process to which God calls all believers, not just those who came to faith as adults. Every member of the Church is on a journey of conversion, he said, and he challenged them to take seriously God's call to continued growth in the Spirit, regardless of how long they had called themselves Christians or Catholics. Since then, Mary has often prayed for the grace to see where God was calling her to change her attitudes and her life. And she rejoices in the small ways that she can see that her life has changed under the influence of God's grace.

QUESTIONS FOR REFLECTION AND DISCUSSION

1. *Have you been aware of your life journey as a continual process of conversion? Does that concept make sense to you?*

2. *Can you name some pivotal moments along your conversion journey, times when you can see significant change in your thinking or behavior?*

3. *Can you recount any times when the proclamation of God's Word triggered another step in your conversion process?*

4. *Can you explain how the liturgy is actually a sharing in the very life of the Trinity? Has your experience of the liturgy led you more deeply into sharing the divine life and mission?*

5. *How has your involvement in the liturgy of the Church shaped your own attitudes and behaviors? What elements of the liturgy seem most powerful in affecting your life?*

6. *How open are you to being changed by God when you come to the liturgy? What hinders that openness? What fosters it in you?*

RESOURCES FOR FURTHER READING

Conn, Walter. *Christian Conversion.* New York/Mahwah: Paulist Press, 1986.

Dunning, James B. "Conversion: Being Born Again and Again and Again," *Catholic Update,* 1988.

Griffin, Emilie. *Turning: Reflections on the Experience of Conversion.* Garden City, NY: Doubleday Image, 1982.

Mick, Lawrence E. *Living Baptism Daily.* Collegeville, MN: The Liturgical Press, 2004.

Morrill, Bruce T. *Anamnesis as Dangerous Memory.* Collegeville, MN: The Liturgical Press, 2000.

Vincie, Catherine. *Celebrating Divine Mystery: A Primer in Liturgical Theology.* Collegeville, MN: The Liturgical Press, 2009.

CHAPTER 7
The Liturgical Year

Since the process of conversion is a lifelong journey, we would not expect any single liturgy to accomplish the task of shaping us into the image of Christ. The liturgy is intended to be celebrated repeatedly, week by week and year by year.

The liturgical year offers us a recurring cycle of seasons and feasts that guide our spiritual journey and lead us more deeply into the mystery of Christ. The Church calendar, as we noted earlier, has variations from country to country, but the basic pattern is the same throughout the world.

The liturgical year has two basic cycles, each of which continues through the whole year. One is a sanctoral cycle, celebrating the feasts of numerous saints throughout the year. Most of these saints will be celebrated on weekdays. The other is a temporal cycle of seasons and feasts of the Lord.

In the recent past, the calendar was almost overwhelmed by the number of saints' feasts in the sanctoral cycle so that the temporal cycle was seldom experienced even on Sunday. The reforms of the calendar after the Second Vatican Council sought to restore the primacy of Sunday itself and to allow the seasons to be more fully celebrated by restricting the number of saints' feasts that can displace the Sunday celebration.

The temporal cycle consists of two major feasts with their accompanying seasons: the Advent-Christmas seasons and the Lent-Triduum-Easter seasons. In between these festal groups, we celebrate Sundays in Ordinary Time.

The liturgical year begins with the season of Advent, starting four Sundays before Christmas. Some people think of Advent as a penitential season very similar to Lent, but Advent is more of an anticipatory season of preparation for Christmas. It is subdued because it is preparatory and contrasts with the joyful exuberance of the Christmas season. The Glory to God is not sung, so it sounds fresh as the song of the angels at the celebration of Christ's birth. We limit the flowers and musical accompaniment so that the joyful sights and sounds of Christmas will signify the shift from preparation to full celebration.

The word "Advent" comes from the Latin for "coming," and the season focuses on the two comings of Christ—his coming in history at Bethlehem and his second coming in glory at the end of time. We are not waiting for him to be born in Bethlehem; that historical event has already occurred, and we recall and celebrate it at Christmas. We wait now for his return, for the coming of the kingdom in its fullness. The readings for the first Sunday of Advent speak of the end of time and remind us that the kingdom is still on the way to fulfillment. At the other end of Advent, we focus on the immediate preparation for Christ's first coming as the feast of his birth approaches.

In between these two comings of Christ, we live in what the theologians call the "already but the not yet." The kingdom of God has already come in Christ, but it is not yet fully present in our world. Thus we yearn for the coming of the kingdom more completely. This suggests that Advent might be a good time for prayer of lament. We voice our lament to God about the state of things in our world, and we cry out for redemption. "We await the blessed hope and the coming of our Savior, Jesus Christ," as we pray in every Mass.

The Christmas season, of course, is the celebration of the birth of Christ at Bethlehem, but it is also much more than that. It is really a celebration of the Incarnation, God taking on human flesh and embracing the human condition. In Jesus, the Son of God shared our humanity fully. This is not just a past event, for the Incarnation continues today. God is found in our midst today, still sharing our humanity and still part of our daily lives. It is this continuing presence of God in our world that we celebrate during the Christmas season. The human and the divine were fully united in Jesus Christ, and that union continues forever. It continues in Christ himself, who is forever the God-man. It also continues in the Church, the body of Christ in the world today. God has entered into our world in such a profound way that nothing has been the same since. That fact is what Christmas celebrates.

The season begins with Christmas Day and continues until the celebration of the Baptism of the Lord. It includes the Feast of the Holy Family on the Sunday between Christmas and New Year's Day, the Solemnity of Mary, the Mother of God on January 1, the Solemnity of the Epiphany on January 6 or the Sunday nearest that date, and the feast of the Baptism of the Lord, usually on the following Sunday. All these feasts fit into the season if we understand it as celebrating Christ's Incarnation. The feast of the Holy Family reminds us that Jesus lived our life and grew up in a human family as most of us do. The celebration of Mary, the Mother of God reminds us that he had a human mother and that he was subject to the religious laws and customs of Israel. Epiphany and the Baptism of the Lord both celebrate Christ's revelation to the world and his mission to redeem all people.

One of the big challenges with this season today (and with Advent) is that our culture focuses attention on Christmas throughout Advent in order to promote sales of gift items, and then drops it almost completely on December 25. In the Church calendar, Christmas begins when the culture drops it. So it takes extra effort on our part, both to keep the spirit of Advent in the midst of the Christmas commercialism and to sustain the celebration of Christmas throughout the season itself.

Between the Christmas season and the beginning of

Lent, we have a few Sundays of Ordinary Time. The exact number changes from year to year because the date of Easter varies, which means the start of Lent varies, too. We'll say more about Ordinary Time a little later.

Lent-Triduum-Easter is the longest and most important festal cycle in the year. It begins with the start of Lent on Ash Wednesday and continues until the celebration of Pentecost at the end of the Easter season. With forty days of Lent, three days of Triduum, and fifty days of Easter, this cycle covers a full quarter of the year.

Lent is a season that many people, even non-Christians, recognize as a time for penance and self-denial. What is not clear to many people is why we do such things during Lent. The key to understanding the season is its link to baptism. Lent is primarily a season for baptismal preparation and baptismal renewal.

During Lent, those adults and children of catechetical age who are preparing for baptism are in their final period of the catechumenate, a period called Purification and Enlightenment. This is a time for spiritual reflection and prayer as they approach the Easter sacraments of initiation (baptism, confirmation, and Eucharist). As they fast and pray in what we might call a six-week retreat, those of us who are already baptized fast and pray to offer our support to their conversion journey. This actually was the origin of Lent as the whole community began to accompany those who were preparing for initiation.

Focusing on those who are about to be baptized naturally leads us to recall our own baptism. At Mass at the

Easter Vigil or on Easter Sunday, all the baptized renew their baptismal promises. So Lent is a time of baptismal preparation for the unbaptized and a time of baptismal renewal for those already baptized. Our efforts at self-denial and spiritual growth during Lent are really ways that we deepen our baptismal commitment and embrace more fully our identity as the baptized. As we recall the suffering and death of the Lord, especially in the latter part of Lent, we remind ourselves that we must die to sin in order to rise to fullness of life in Christ.

Triduum is a Latin term meaning "the three days." It refers to the three central days of the whole liturgical year. The Triduum lasts from the evening of Holy Thursday until the evening of Easter Sunday. To many people, that sounds like four days, but the days are counted in the Jewish fashion from sundown to sundown. So Holy Thursday night and Good Friday are one day; Good Friday night and Holy Saturday mark the second day; Holy Saturday night, when the Easter Vigil is celebrated, and Easter Sunday constitute the third day.

The Triduum is not part of Lent. Lent ends before the evening Mass of the Lord's Supper on Holy Thursday. Yet our fasting intensifies with the paschal fast, which is obligatory on Friday but strongly encouraged on Saturday (that really means Thursday night through Saturday afternoon). This fast helps us prepare our hearts by focusing our attention on the great feast ahead.

The three main liturgies of the Triduum are the Evening Mass of the Lord's Supper on Thursday, the Commemoration of the Passion on Good Friday, and the Easter Vigil on Holy Saturday night. These are the "high holy days" of the Christian faith. All members of the Church should try to take part in these liturgies, especially in the Easter Vigil.

The Easter Vigil is the central liturgy of the whole year. People still call parish offices to find out if it "counts" for Easter. It is THE Easter Mass. If everyone could gather for that central celebration, we would not even need any Masses on Easter Sunday morning. This is the night that the Church is renewed by initiating new members. This is the primary celebration of the resurrection of the Lord Jesus, as we see new members of his body go through the watery tomb and emerge into resurrection life. This is the night we all recall our history as a people and our personal history as members of the Church since our own baptisms. There is no liturgy more central or more beautiful than the Easter Vigil.

Easter begins with Easter Sunday and continues for fifty days until the celebration of Pentecost. Sometimes this is called the Easter season, but it is also called simply "Easter," recognizing it as a fifty-day celebration of the resurrection. That is why the Sunday after Easter Sunday is called the Second Sunday *of* Easter, not the first Sunday *after* Easter. As the *General Norms for the Liturgical Year and the Liturgical Calendar* say, "The fifty days from Easter Sunday to Pentecost are celebrated in joyful exultation as one feast day or better as one 'great Sunday' "(22).

Easter is a time to rejoice in the new life we share because of the resurrection of Christ. The newly baptized, sometimes called *neophytes*, spend this time reflecting on the meaning of the sacraments they received at the Vigil. This period of their formation is called *mystagogy*, from the Greek term that means "the study of the mysteries." Mystery is an ancient term for sacrament.

This mystagogy is carried out primarily at the Easter Sunday Masses. The readings for those Masses offer numerous opportunities to reflect together on what it means to be baptized in Christ, confirmed in the Spirit, and sharing at the Lord's table. This reflection is not for the neophytes alone, however. All the baptized should share in this common reflection, since it is supposed to be prompted by the preaching at the Sunday Masses of Easter. This is a season for all members of the assembly to rejoice in the new life they share and to deepen their appreciation for what this new life entails on a day-to-day basis.

After Pentecost, we return to Ordinary Time until Advent arrives again. This is the longest stretch of the year, lasting from seven to eight months. Calling it Ordinary Time is a bit of a misnomer. The Latin title would be more accurately translated as "Ordinal," meaning counted. We designate these weeks as the Tenth Sunday or the Twenty-seventh Sunday of Ordinary Time, so they are the "counted Sundays." On the other hand, compared to the two great festal seasons, we do experience these weeks as more ordinary, too.

During this season, the Gospel readings present us with the teaching and the miracles of Christ during his earthly ministry. It is a time to allow ourselves to be guided by Christ's words and example as we live out the Christian life. If Advent-Christmas recalls the beginning of his life on earth, and Lent-Triduum-Easter celebrates his death and resurrection, then Ordinary Time allows us to walk with him through his public ministry.

It is important to recognize, as Pope Pius XII taught in his 1943 encyclical, *Mediator Dei*, that "the liturgical year...is not a cold and lifeless representation of the events of the past, or a simple and bare record of a former age. It is rather Christ Himself who is ever living in His Church. Here He continues that journey of immense mercy which He lovingly began in His mortal life, going about doing good, with the design of bringing men to know His mysteries and in a way live by them" (165).

We don't celebrate the many events of Christ's life in the liturgical year just to recall what happened long ago, but to be caught up in the mystery of his life and his presence among us. When we celebrate his death and resurrection, we are invited to make his attitude our own, to seek the Father's will as completely as he did, regardless of the cost. We are reminded of the need for each of us to die to selfishness and sin so that we can live more fully the risen life of the redeemed.

When we celebrate his birth as a poor and helpless baby, we are invited to deepen our awareness that he continues to live in his people today so that we will recognize him in those we meet, especially the poor and the needy. We are also invited to bring him forth to the world today as Mary did in her time, to reveal his presence to the world through our love and service of others in union with Christ.

When we listen to his teaching or hear of his compassion toward the sick and the disabled, we are invited to live those teachings and follow his example. In every part of the liturgical year, Christ is present urging us to share his life, embrace his values, and love others as he loves us.

JOE'S JOURNEY

When Joe first approached the parish about becoming Catholic, he was surprised (and a bit hesitant, he admits today) to discover that the process would take at least a full year. That seemed like a long time to wait for baptism. But now it's been more than a year, and Joe says he still has a lot to learn. Through that first year, Joe was fascinated by the many different feasts and seasons that the parish celebrated. Some were familiar, of course; almost everybody knows something about Christmas and Easter. But others were new to him. He found Advent an interesting contrast to society's focus on shopping and partying before Christmas. He's looking forward to Lent next year, because he expects to be ready then to enter into his final preparation for celebrating the sacraments of initiation at Easter. As he has lived through the year with the parish community, he has come to value the different seasons as ways to enter more fully into the life of Christ. He has also learned a bit about a number of the saints that the catechumenate team has lifted up as examples of those who have lived the faith fully in ages past. He finds himself especially drawn to Saint Francis of Assisi, because he loves being outdoors and he thinks that care for the environment is an important moral issue in our own time.

MARY'S JOURNEY

Mary grew up with the feasts and seasons of the Church year, so they are very familiar to her. She remembers a time, though, when a different saint was celebrated almost every day at Mass, even on Sundays. In recent years, she has become more aware of the importance of the Sunday itself and of the power of the various seasons to draw her more fully into the mystery of God's life. She sometimes misses the emphasis on the saints that marked her early life, so she makes a point of praying to those saints on their feast days as they occur throughout the week. She has also noticed that some of the seasons are a bit different now than when she was young. Advent, for example, used to seem like just a shorter version of Lent; now she sees it as a time of yearning for the coming of the kingdom. In Lent, she used to focus mostly on the sufferings and death of Christ. Since she served a few years ago as a sponsor for a woman joining the Church, she has come to see Lent more as a time of prayer and support for those preparing for baptism and a time for renewing her own baptismal commitment. And she has really come to look forward to the season of Easter, fifty days of joy and celebration of the resurrection.

QUESTIONS FOR REFLECTION AND DISCUSSION

1. *How would you explain the purpose of the liturgical year?*

2. *Can you explain the meaning of the Advent-Christmas cycle? What is celebrated in the Lent-Triduum-Easter cycle?*

3. *Is the shift in liturgical seasons evident in your community's worship, through decor, music, etc.? What would help you to be more aware of the various seasons and feasts?*

4. *Do you celebrate the liturgies of the Triduum: Holy Thursday, Good Friday, and Easter Vigil? Have you ever experienced these liturgies? Why or why not?*

5. *What part of the Church year do you find most meaningful or spiritually fruitful? Why?*

6. *What can you do to enter more fully into each of the seasons of the year? What might your community do to foster deeper engagement in the various seasons and feasts?*

RESOURCES FOR FURTHER READING

Adam, Adolph. *The Liturgical Year: Its History and Its Meaning After the Reform of the Liturgy.* Collegeville, MN: The Liturgical Press, 1992.

Between Memory and Hope: Readings on the Liturgical Year. Johnson, Maxwell E., ed. Collegeville, MN: The Liturgical Press, 2000.

Biffi, Inos. *An Introduction to the Liturgical Year.* Chicago: Liturgy Training Publications, 2007.

Bogle, Joanna. *A Yearbook of Seasons and Celebrations.* Chicago: Liturgy Training Publications, 2007.

Connell, Martin. *An Introduction to the Church's Liturgical Year.* Chicago: Loyola Press, 1997.

Irwin, Kevin. *Sunday Worship: A Planning Guide to Celebration.* New York: Pueblo Publishing, 1983.

Martimort, Aimé Georges; Irénée Henri Dalmais, Pierre Jounel. *The Church at Prayer: Volume IV: The Liturgy and Time.* Collegeville, MN: The Liturgical Press, 1986, Sections 1 & 2.

Talley, Thomas J. *The Origins of the Liturgical Year.* Collegeville, MN: The Liturgical Press, 1986, 1991.

The Liturgical Year: Celebrating the Mystery of Christ and His Saints, Study Text 9. Washington, DC: United States Conference of Catholic Bishops, 1985.

PART THREE

Enacting the Ritual

CHAPTER 8
Do This in Memory of Me

In each of the sacraments, after we have gathered and shared the Word of God, we enact a central ritual action that forms the core of the sacrament. In baptism we bring people to and through the waters of the font to initiate them into the Church community. In holy orders, we set aside and consecrate men to serve the Church as deacons, priests, or bishops. In the anointing of the sick, we anoint the seriously ill and surround them with the prayerful support of the Church community as we urge them to unite their sufferings with those of Christ.

For simplicity of discussion, we will focus here on the eucharistic meal that forms the core of our central sacrament, but much of what is said will apply with minimal adjustment to the other sacramental liturgies.

As we noted earlier, symbols are better understood as actions rather than objects. We do things with various objects (bread, wine, water, oil), and it is the use of these things that constitutes the sacramental ritual. At the Last Supper, Jesus told his disciples not just to remember him, but also to "do this" in his memory.

Ever since, his followers have celebrated the eucharistic meal in his memory. Sharing consecrated bread and wine is the core ritual of the Eucharist, even though it is certainly a simple meal. It consists of only bread and wine—and each person receives a very small amount to eat and drink. This is clearly a *symbolic* meal. It reminds us that simple symbols can represent much larger realities. It also reminds us that it is not just the objects but the actions that really matter. The symbol here is the *sharing* of bread and wine, not just the bread and wine on their own. This is not to say that the material symbols are unimportant, but simply to remember that they draw their full meaning from how they are used in the ritual.

The Liturgy of the Eucharist, as the second main part of the Mass is called, consists of three sections: the Preparation of the Gifts, the Eucharistic Prayer, and Communion. We might describe these as setting the table for the meal, saying the blessing, and sharing the meal together.

The Preparation of the Gifts is not a major section of the ritual, but it does have some rich symbolic meaning. Here the bread and wine and our monetary donations serve as symbols of our gifts and of ourselves. The collection gathered for the needs of the Church and the poor, which is brought forward with the bread and wine, speaks of our willingness to follow the Lord in caring for those in need. It also reminds us that all that we have, not just that portion we put in the basket, belongs to God. The donations we make symbolize all that we have and ultimately all that we are. Our giving symbolizes our commitment to give our whole lives to God and to use all the gifts God has given us according to God's will. The presentation of the gifts from the assembly reminds us that we are all involved in this act of worship, presider and assembly together. As the gifts and the altar are prepared, so we prepare ourselves to enter into the great blessing prayer and the meal that is to follow.

The Eucharistic Prayer is the central prayer of the liturgy. The word "eucharist" comes from the Greek for "thanksgiving," and this prayer is primarily an act of praise and thanks to God for all that God has done for us through the ages. It is a descendent of Jewish prayer forms like the *berakah*. The *berakah* prayer begins with a stylized blessing of God (e.g., "Blessed are you, Lord our God, Creator of all") and recalls the reasons for blessing God (which means praising and thanking God). Then the prayer asks God to continue to bless us in our own time and concludes with words of praise (a doxology).

We can see this same pattern in the Eucharistic Prayer. We begin with a standard formula: "Lift up your hearts. *We lift them up to the Lord.* Let us give thanks to the Lord our God. *It is right to give him thanks and praise.*" (New missal: "Lift up your hearts. *We lift them up to the Lord.* Let us give thanks to the Lord our God. *It is right and just.*") Then we recall what God has done for us throughout salvation history, sometimes briefly, sometimes more fully. This always includes what God has done through Jesus and culminates in his death and resurrection. Then we pray for the Church, for the living and for the dead, and finally we conclude with the doxology: "Through him and with him and in him...."

Many people find it difficult to sustain their attention through the length of this prayer. Though it may help if presiders learned to sing the prayer more often, probably the most important thing is for all the worshippers to remember that they are offering this prayer together with the presider. The opening dialogue and the three acclamations that the assembly sings as part of the prayer (Holy, Memorial Acclamation, Great Amen) are reminders that this is a communal effort to give God proper praise and thanks.

In the Catholic tradition, we believe that this prayer is also consecratory. The prayer is said over the bread and wine that have been set aside for the sacred meal, and through this prayer, the bread and wine become the Body and Blood of Christ. The word "transubstantiation" has traditionally been used to express this change; it simply says that the substance or fundamental reality of the bread and wine change even though the "accidents," what we see and touch and taste, remain the same. What is more basic than the term, however, is the truth that the bread and wine are now the Body and Blood of the Lord, which means they are now a bodily means of his presence among us. He is present in the Eucharist just as fully as he was present in his human body during his thirty-plus years on earth.

He is present for a purpose. He is present in the Eucharist in order to be our spiritual food and drink. The communion rite brings the meal to its climax, as the assembly shares together the Body and Blood of the Lord in a deep and intimate Communion, the moment of the greatest unity of the body of Christ. There are several moments of immediate preparation for Communion in the ritual. The assembly prays together the Lord's Prayer, praying for daily bread and committing themselves to mutual forgiveness. They share a sign of peace, wishing each other the peace of Christ and reminding themselves of the unity Christ intends for all the members of his body. The bread is broken and prepared for sharing. This practical ritual carried enough symbolic weight that it gave its name to the whole celebration in the early Church; they called it "the breaking of the bread," because the breaking and sharing expressed their unity in the one loaf and the one body of Christ.

Remember, too, that Jesus told us to eat and to drink, to share his body and his blood. The normal way of sharing a meal involves both food and drink, and the normal form of Communion for most of the Church's history has been to share both bread and cup. After a controversy about whether Christ was really received if someone received only the bread or only the cup, the Church tried to reinforce its teaching that Christ is fully received even in one species by offering only the bread to the laity. There was some effort to return to the practice of both species in the sixteenth century, but when the Protestant churches adopted the practice, the Catholic Church decided to stay with one species. The Second Vatican Council decided to restore the practice of both species in our own time, a return to what Jesus clearly intended. While receiving under both species is not mandatory, it is a fuller sign of Communion with the Lord.

> Holy Communion has a fuller form as a sign when it is distributed under both kinds. For in this form the sign of a eucharistic banquet is more clearly evident and clear expression is given to the divine will by which the new and eternal Covenant is ratified in the Blood of the Lord, as also the relationship between the Eucharistic banquet and the eschatological banquet in the Father's Kingdom. (GIRM, #281)

JOE'S JOURNEY

As a catechumen, Joe is dismissed from Mass each Sunday after the homily. Though he had been present for the second half of the Mass a few times before he decided to join the Church, he has had little experience of the Eucharistic Prayer so far. Nevertheless, the themes of this prayer have been a vital part of his catechumenal formation. Several catechists have helped the catechumens to reflect on all the ways that God has blessed them, so that they have been growing in their sense of gratitude to God. When they arrive for their catechumenal sessions, there is usually a table with a candle or a Bible or some other items on it. Sometimes that has included bread and wine, and those sessions began with a prayer of thanksgiving for those gifts. They have also been taught to begin meals at home with prayer, thanking God for the food and drink that sustain their lives and for all the ways God blesses them. Their study of the Bible in the course of the year also included the Scripture accounts of the Last Supper, and Joe knows that he will be a full member of the Church when he is able to share at the table of the Lord.

MARY'S JOURNEY

Mary has been staying for the whole Mass ever since she can remember. She deeply values the opportunity to share in Communion at each Mass. The Eucharistic Prayer, however, has been a challenge for her. In her youth, she said her rosary while the priest said the prayer silently. When the priest started saying the prayer aloud in English, she learned to listen to it, but she still finds that her mind wanders sometimes in the midst of the prayer, simply because it is a long prayer. She has learned not to worry too much about that, but simply to do the best she can to stay tuned in. One thing that has helped her is learning that the prayer is really being offered by all the people gathered, not just by the priest. She tries now to really make the prayer her own, enthusiastically expressing her affirmation of the priest's words by singing the Holy, the Memorial Acclamation, and the Great Amen. Another change in the Mass that she has welcomed is receiving both the Body and Blood of Christ at Communion. Even though she knows the Lord is fully present in each species, it makes sense to her that we should do as Jesus told us—to eat his Body and drink his Blood.

QUESTIONS FOR REFLECTION AND DISCUSSION

1. *What makes it easy for you to recognize the Eucharist as a meal? What makes it difficult? Why do you think Jesus chose the meal as the symbol for this central sacrament?*

2. *Does the Preparation of the Gifts help you prepare to enter into the Eucharistic Prayer and Communion? What role does the collection play in that process?*

3. *What is your experience of the Eucharistic Prayer? Do you pray it as your own prayer, as the assembly's prayer? What would help you to enter more deeply into this central prayer of the Mass?*

4. *How would you explain to someone else the Church's belief in the change of the bread and wine into the Body and Blood of Christ?*

5. *What is the ultimate purpose of the Eucharist? Have you found your sharing in the Eucharist leading to that result?*

6. *Do you receive Communion under both species of bread and wine? If not, why not? Can you explain the symbolic meanings attached to each form?*

RESOURCES FOR FURTHER READING

Mazza, Enrico. *The Eucharistic Prayers of the Roman Rite*. Collegeville, MN: The Liturgical Press, 1986.

McCarron, Richard. *The Eucharistic Prayer at Sunday Mass*. Chicago: Liturgy Training Publications, 1997.

Rech, Photina. *Wine and Bread*. Chicago: Liturgy Training Publications, 1998.

CHAPTER 9
The Paschal Mystery

The Liturgy of the Eucharist is the basic ritual that Jesus commanded his followers to do in his memory. Of course, doing "this" in memory of Jesus really entails far more than sharing the eucharistic meal. It means living out the meaning of the ritual, too. The core of that meaning is summed up in the term "paschal mystery." This refers to the death and resurrection of the Lord and to our sharing in his death and new life. The word "paschal" refers to the Passover. Through his death, Jesus passed over from this life into resurrected life. This is the core mystery of the Christian faith.

If it is central to the Christian life, then the paschal mystery will logically be central to the liturgy as well. Each of the sacraments brings us into contact with this mystery and invites us to enter into it. The Eucharist, as our central sacrament, offers us our most frequent ritual contact with this central mystery of our faith.

We are first immersed in the paschal mystery at our baptism. In that initial sacrament, we enter the watery tomb to die with Christ and rise from the waters to live a new life. From this sacramental death until our final death when we leave this world, our lives are to be marked by this dynamic of dying to sin and rising to new life. Over and over again, we confront the choice of whether we will act in selfishness or embrace the love of Christ. Each time that we die to selfishness, we move a bit more fully into the new life that we embraced at baptism. As we move through life, the sacraments continue to celebrate this mystery and bring us into contact with it so that we will be drawn more deeply into its dynamic. Marriage and holy orders, for example, call us to live out our baptismal commitment in particular vocations, dying to self to live for others. Penance calls us to renew our baptismal commitment, dying again to sin and being reconciled with God and embracing again our life in Christ. Anointing of the sick invites us to enter into the paschal mystery with our own suffering that we might more fully embrace new life.

The dynamic of the paschal mystery provides the template for a unified understanding of the Christian faith. Everything we do as a Church and everything we believe and teach is linked to this mystery. Our moral theology is ultimately a systematic attempt to understand what dying to sin and living Christ's life looks like in practice. The various schools of spirituality in the Church are different ways of trying to intensify our rejection of sin and our embrace of life in Christ Jesus. All our pious practices and efforts at self-discipline aim to help us in that process. Our catechetical efforts are ultimately aimed at leading people to a deeper appreciation of this mystery so that they will live it out in their daily lives. While all the various activities of the Church can seem disconnected at times, they begin to make sense if we view them from the perspective of this central mystery.

If we first embrace the dying and rising of Christ in baptism, it is in the Eucharist that we have regular contact with it sacramentally. The Eucharist calls us to enter into the sacrifice of Christ, to offer that sacrifice to the Father in union with Christ. Catholics have long spoken of the Mass as a sacrifice, yet the New Testament Letter to the Hebrews is very clear that there is only one sacrifice in the New Covenant. Only one is necessary, and only one is acceptable—that of Christ himself. So if the Mass is a sacrifice, it must somehow be the one unique sacrifice of Christ.

That can be difficult to understand if we think only of the historical circumstances in which his sacrifice was manifested on Calvary. Those historical events are part of the past. Christ died once for all, and he dies no more. Death has no more power over him, Saint Paul insists (see Romans 6:9). Yet we are invited to share in the sacrifice of Christ, a sacrifice that is described as eternal. The eternal dimension of his sacrifice might be best recognized in the agony in the garden before his arrest and crucifixion. He begged his Father that the cup of suffering might be taken away from him, but ultimately he prayed, "...not my will but yours be done" (Luke 22:42). This is the core of his sacrifice, uniting his will with the

Father's will. This is what endures through all eternity; Christ is forever victim, forever priest. His will is always in complete accord with the Father's will. That commitment led him to the cross because he could not avoid it and still stay faithful to the mission the Father had given him. For us, the way that faithfulness will be expressed will be different, but we are called to the same commitment.

This is the sacrifice we celebrate in every Eucharist. This is the sacrifice we are invited to share. We do so to the extent that we take on the same attitude as Christ, to the extent that we align our own wills with the Father's will. It is this that Christ told us to "do in memory of" him. Doing the ritual in his memory is intended to lead us to living out its meaning in his memory. When we sing "Amen" at the end of the Eucharistic Prayer, we are signifying our willingness to imitate what we have just recalled of the life, death, and resurrection of our Savior. It is not a response we should make lightly, for it may cost us our life!

JOE'S JOURNEY

When Joe formally entered the catechumenate through the rite of Acceptance into the Order of Catechumens, the sign of the cross was traced on his forehead, his ears, his eyes, his lips, his heart, his shoulders, his hands, and his feet. That was a dramatic and powerful expression of the centrality of the cross in the catechumenate formation and in the whole Christian life. Since that time, Joe has been learning to see his life in terms of the cross and the promise of resurrection that it holds. He finds it easier now to see the difficulties of life as an opportunity to die to self and to live more fully in Christ. And he can point to various times in his life when what seemed like a completely negative experience actually led him to growth in his faith in God or his ability to love others unselfishly. That theme of dying and rising has appeared constantly during the catechumenate, in catechesis and in prayer, in opportunities for service and in times of reflection. Joe has learned that following Christ always entails carrying the cross, but he knows that this is the way to fuller life in Christ, too.

MARY'S JOURNEY

Mary has always been very aware of the necessity of carrying the cross as part of the Christian life. She remembers being told often in her youth to "offer up" her sufferings in union with Christ, and her early experiences of Lent focused almost totally on the sufferings and death of Jesus. In those years, though, the resurrection received much less emphasis. The renewal of the liturgy after the Second Vatican Council led her to see the importance of the resurrection and to link it more closely to the crucifixion. She now thinks of them as two sides of the same coin.

The day that the paschal mystery really impressed itself on her consciousness was the day her husband, Paul, was buried. The funeral liturgy began by recalling Paul's baptism, the first time he died and rose with Christ, and it concluded with entrusting him to God's love in the hope of final resurrection in union with the Lord. Ever since that day, Mary has been looking forward to the day when God calls her home, too, so that she can be with Paul again. In the meantime, she relies on the promise of resurrection whenever she senses God's call to her to die a bit more to her sinfulness and live more fully in Christ.

QUESTIONS FOR REFLECTION AND DISCUSSION

1. *Can you explain the meaning of the term "paschal mystery"? To what degree does it serve as a template for your life and spiritual growth?*

2. *How do the different sacraments draw us more deeply into the paschal mystery?*

3. *How does the paschal mystery shape the other parts of the Church's life?*

4. *Can you explain how Christ's sacrifice is eternal? How can we share in his unique sacrifice?*

5. *What do you think Jesus meant when he told his disciples to "do this" in his memory?*

Resources for Further Reading

Campbell, Stanislaus. "The Paschal Mystery in the Eucharistic Prayer," http://www.naal-liturgy.org/seminars/formation/campbell2001.pdf.

Catechism of the Catholic Church (Washington, DC: USCC, 1994), nn. 1066-1209.

Chauvet, Louis-Marie. *The Sacraments: The Word of God at the Mercy of the Body.* Collegeville, MN: The Liturgical Press, 2001, esp. chapter 8.

Hunt, Anne. *The Trinity and the Paschal Mystery.* Collegeville, MN: The Liturgical Press, 1997.

Lash, Nicholas. *His Presence in the World: A Study of Eucharistic Worship and Theology.* Dayton, OH: Pflaum Press, 1968.

O'Connor, Roc. "The Threat of the Paschal Mystery," http://www.naal-liturgy.org/seminars/formation/oconnor2002.pdf.

Stevenson, Kenneth. *Accept This Sacrifice: The Eucharist as Sacrifice Today.* Collegeville, MN: The Liturgical Press, 1989.

CHAPTER 10
The Challenge of Communion

If all those who have gathered together for worship unite their wills with the Father's will, then they will be of one mind and one heart as they approach the table of the Lord. For some worshippers, this may be the first test of whether they have really embraced the attitude of Christ. Being willing to be in intimate communion with all the members of Christ's body who share the eucharistic meal can be a difficult challenge. Yet it is to this unity that the Eucharist calls us.

This should be obvious from the very word we use for the culmination of the sacrament. We call it Communion, expressing union with Christ and with all the members of his body. This union is the main purpose of this sacrament. This truth has been attested throughout the centuries of Christian history. Saint Paul insists that if we eat and drink the Body and the Blood without recognizing the body, we eat and drink a condemnation to ourselves (see 1 Corinthians 11:29). Saint Augustine in the fifth century chastised his people for wanting to decapitate Christ, thinking they could receive the head without the body. We must receive the whole Christ, he insisted. Saint Thomas Aquinas in the thirteenth century taught that the ultimate purpose of the Eucharist was the unity of the Church. Pope John Paul II, in his encyclical on the Eucharist, quotes both Saint Paul and Saint John Chrysostom:

> Eucharistic communion also confirms the Church in her unity as the Body of Christ. Saint Paul refers to this *unifying power* of participation in the banquet of the Eucharist when he writes to the Corinthians: "The bread which we break, is it not a communion in the body of Christ? Because there is one bread, we who are many are one body, for we all partake of the one bread" (1 Cor. 10:16–17). Saint John Chrysostom's commentary on these words is profound and perceptive: "For what is the bread? It is the body of Christ. And what do those who receive it become? The Body of Christ—not many bodies but one body. For as bread is completely one, though made up of many grains of wheat, and these, albeit unseen, remain nonetheless present in such a way that their difference is not apparent since they have been made a perfect whole, so too are we mutually joined to one another and together united with Christ." The argument is compelling: our union with Christ, which is a gift and grace for each of us, makes it possible for us, in him, to share in the

unity of his body which is the Church. The Eucharist reinforces the incorporation into Christ
which took place in baptism through the gift of
the Spirit (cf. 1 Cor 12:13, 27).

ECCLESIA DE EUCHARISTIA, 23

This relationship between the sacramental body of
Christ and the ecclesial or mystical body is key to a proper understanding of the Eucharist. Here lies the heart of
the mystery of this sacrament: the body of Christ receives
the Body of Christ to become more fully united as the
body of Christ. As Saint Augustine put it, "It is your own
mystery that is placed upon the altar....You reply 'Amen'
to that which you are, and by replying you consent. For
you hear 'The Body of Christ' and you reply 'Amen'....
Be what you see, and receive what you are" (Sermon
272). The well-known Trappist monk, Thomas Merton,
said it well: "We will never appreciate the Real Presence
fully until we see the intimate connection which exists
between the Mystery of the Eucharist and the Mystery of
the Church, two sacred realities which completely inter-
penetrate to form a single whole; Mysteries which, when
separated, elude the grasp of our spirit altogether. For we
will never really appreciate the Eucharist or the Church
if we conceive them to be two entirely different 'bodies
of Christ'" (*The Living Bread*, p. 133). It is interesting
to note that for the first thousand years of the Church's
history, when people spoke of the "real body" of Christ,
they meant the Church, and they called the sacramental

body the "mystical body" of Christ. In the past thousand years, we have reversed the terms, calling the Church the mystical body of Christ. One might argue for either pattern, but the history reminds us that these two forms of Christ's bodily presence are intimately related.

Here we can also recognize the close connection between Eucharist and baptism. We become part of the Body of Christ at baptism, and the Eucharist continually reinforces our identity as members of that body. It reminds us over and over again that we are linked to one another in Christ. The Eucharist seeks to intensify our unity every time we gather, which should not be a surprise if we read John's account of the Lord's discourse during the Last Supper. Jesus speaks over and over about his will that we be united. "I ask not only on behalf of these, but also on behalf of those who will believe in me through their word, that they may all be one. As you, Father, are in me and I am in you, may they also be in us, so that the world may believe that you have sent me" (John 17:20–21).

The source of this unity is the Holy Spirit, whom we receive in baptism and confirmation. In the Eucharistic Prayer, we pray that the power of the Spirit will come upon the bread and wine to transform them into the Body and Blood of Christ. But we also pray, right after the narrative of the Last Supper, that this same Spirit will transform us into the body of Christ. "May all of us who share in the body and blood of Christ be brought together in unity by the Holy Spirit." (New missal: "Humbly we pray that, partaking of the Body and Blood of Christ, we may be gathered into one by the Holy Spirit.") [Eucharistic Prayer II]. "Grant that we, who are nourished by his body and blood, may be filled with his Holy Spirit, and become one body, one spirit in Christ." (New missal: "...grant that we, who are nourished by the Body and Blood of your Son and filled with his Holy Spirit, may become one body, one spirit in Christ.") [Eucharistic Prayer III]. "Lord, look upon this sacrifice which you have given to your Church; and by your Holy Spirit, gather all who share this one bread and one cup into the one body of Christ, a living sacrifice of praise." (New missal: "Look, O Lord, upon the Sacrifice which you yourself have provided for your Church, and grant in your loving kindness to all who partake of this one Bread and one Chalice that, gathered into one body by the Holy Spirit, they may truly become a living sacrifice in Christ to the praise of your glory.") [Eucharistic Prayer IV].

The Spirit we invoke is the Spirit of unity, the love that unites the Father and the Son. In baptism and confirmation we are drawn into that divine love and unity, and in every Eucharist, God seeks to draw us more deeply into that unity. Sharing the unity of the Trinity also unites us to all those who are caught up in the same mystery of divine love. That unity finds its fullest ritual expression in the Communion Rite.

The communion procession, as it is intended to be carried out, expresses this unity in two ways. The first is that we are all to sing the communion song throughout the procession. It is to begin when the presider receives Communion and continue until the last person has received. The second is that we are all supposed to maintain a common posture during the procession, which means that we all remain standing until all have received the Body and Blood of the Lord (see *GIRM* 42). We are all part of the procession until it is completed, and we all unite our voices throughout the sharing in the meal.

Then, when all have received, the liturgy offers a time for silence. When the procession ends, all are seated (or all may kneel if that is the parish's practice) and enter into a shared silence for personal prayer. Though many Catholics were trained to enter into that quiet prayer as soon as they returned to their seats, the proper time for it is after all have shared the bread and the cup.

While unity sounds like a wonderful ideal, it is not achieved without cost, nor is it automatically created by receiving the Body and Blood of the Lord. Saint Augustine challenges his people and us, "Be then a member of the Body of Christ that your 'Amen' may be true." What we express symbolically in the Eucharist, we have to live out in daily life. If we are united with all the members of Christ's body at Mass, we must live in unity with them throughout the week as well.

That can be a particularly difficult challenge for a culture that values individuality and personal freedom as much as ours does. Most of us are not used to thinking of ourselves as intimately connected with the people around us, yet our faith teaches us that we are branches on one vine, even though we may not personally know all the other branches. The liturgy seeks to teach us who we really are in God's sight. It continually reminds us that we are baptized, that we have died with Christ and risen to new life, that we are members of the Body of Christ, and that we are called to take his presence wherever we go.

JOE'S JOURNEY

As he has progressed through the catechumenate, Joe has found his desire for the Eucharist growing. While he greatly values the discussions that the catechumens have together when they are dismissed from the Mass, he longs for the time when they will be able to stay and share in the banquet that sustains the whole community. That desire to be part of the assembly that shares the Body and Blood of the Lord gives him a natural understanding of the meaning of Communion. He has come to feel a real part of the parish community as he has gotten to know more and more of the members of the parish and has shared with them in various parish activities. He wants to be fully united with the assembly in their moment of greatest unity in Christ.

MARY'S JOURNEY

For Mary, coming to really understand Communion has been a long journey. As a child, she had been taught to ignore everyone around her when she received Communion and to focus only on her personal relationship with Jesus. When the renewed liturgy included a communion song, she felt that it intruded on the quiet time she needed to commune intimately with Jesus right after she received the Body and Blood. It took her a while to become comfortable with the idea that the whole assembly should sing the song until everyone had received. Only then do they enter together into a time of silence for quiet prayer. Mary finds it helpful that the pastor gives them a significant time of silence after the communion procession is finished. Over time, Mary has come to appreciate the sense of unity that the song expresses while all are sharing at the table of the Lord. In her parish, this sense of unity has been heightened since the whole assembly stays standing until the procession finishes so that they share a common posture as well as a common song.

QUESTIONS FOR REFLECTION AND DISCUSSION

1. *How would you explain the meaning of Communion? Is this a challenge for you to embrace fully?*

2. *What is the connection between the sacramental Body of Christ and the mystical Body of Christ? Are you usually aware of this connection when you receive Communion?*

3. *Why is the Eucharist called the repeatable sacrament of initiation? How does it reinforce baptism and confirmation?*

4. *Can you explain the role of the Holy Spirit in the Eucharist? How aware are you of the Spirit's presence and action in the sacraments—and in your daily life?*

5. *How is the communion procession carried out in your community? Can you see why maintaining a common posture and singing the communion song are appropriate at this moment of unity?*

6. *Does your presider allow a significant time of silence after the communion procession (and the song) is completed? What do you do with this time?*

RESOURCES FOR FURTHER READING

Mahony, Cardinal Roger. *Gathered Faithfully Together: Guide for Sunday Mass.* Chicago: Liturgy Training Publications, 1997.

McCormick, Patrick T. *A Banqueter's Guide to the All-Night Soup Kitchen of the Kingdom of God.* Collegeville, MN: The Liturgical Press, 2004.

McKenna, John. *The Eucharistic Epiclesis: A Detailed History from the Patristic to the Modern Era.* Chicago: Liturgy Training Publications, 2008.

Mick, Lawrence E. "Finding Jesus in the Eucharist: Four Ways He is Present," *Catholic Update,* 2005.

Mitchell, Nathan. *Real Presence: The Work of Eucharist.* Chicago: Liturgy Training Publications, 1998.

PART FOUR

Sending Forth God's People

CHAPTER 11
Sent on Mission

The mission we are given to take Christ to the world and show his love to those we meet is expressed by the final, rather short section of the liturgy. As every communal experience begins with people gathering, so it must end with some kind of leave-taking or dismissal.

The Dismissal Rite of the Eucharist consists of several brief elements. After the prayer that concludes the communion rite, there is time for parish announcements. Then a simple greeting introduces a blessing of the assembly. A brief formula of dismissal is usually followed by a closing song, though such a song is not strictly a part of the ritual.

The placement of the announcements at this point in the liturgy reminds us of the links between worship and daily life. They offer members of the assembly ways that they can live out through the week the commitment they have made during the Eucharist to imitate the Lord Jesus. It might be helpful if parish leaders worded the announcements to make this connection clearer, for example: "As we have shared this holy meal, we invite you to help on Friday to provide food for the needy at the parish soup kitchen."

The blessing and actual dismissal send us forth to carry on the mission of Christ that is now entrusted to us. The actual language of the dismissal is instructive. In Latin, the words are *"Ite, missa est."* This is difficult to translate into English, but a literal translation might be, "Go, it is the dismissal" or "Go, it is the sending." Notice that *missa* is related to our English word "mission." At the end of the liturgy, we are sent forth on mission. The liturgy does not exist for itself but to sustain us in living the Gospel throughout the week. In fact, the term "Mass" comes from *missa*, an interesting fact that can remind us that the liturgy is strongly linked to mission.

The separation of church and state in the United States perhaps makes it harder for us to recognize the links between liturgy and the rest of life. There is a tendency in modern society to see religion as separate from other areas of life. Preachers who attempt to speak the Gospel to the issues of our time are often criticized and told to stay in their own realm and not talk about politics or economics or labor issues or environmental problems or justice questions. And too many people tend to think of Sunday worship as an hour largely divorced from their "real" lives of work and business and social interactions.

Yet the Gospel has little meaning and the liturgy has little purpose if both are divorced from "real" life. Jesus came to teach us how to live in union with God and with one another. Our commitment to follow his teaching and his example, which we reaffirm whenever we celebrate the liturgy, must have implications for every other part of our lives.

It is interesting to note that those who promoted liturgical renewal in the early part of the twentieth century in the United States assumed an intimate link between liturgy and justice. They saw the liturgy as the way that members of the Church could be renewed in the truths of the Gospel, so that they could then contribute more effectively to the transformation of society. One of those early promoters of renewal was Virgil Michel, a Benedictine monk of Saint John's Abbey in Collegeville, Minnesota. In 1936, he wrote, "If the first purpose of the liturgical movement is to lead the faithful into more intimate participation in the liturgy of the Church, then the further objective must also be that of getting the liturgical spirit to radiate forth from the altar of Christ into every aspect of the daily life of the Christian" (*Orate Fratres* 10, 485).

The difficulty of implementing the liturgical reforms following the Second Vatican Council led many people to forget Michel's "further objective." It is certainly important that the members of the Church be taught to participate fully in the liturgy itself. The Constitution on the Sacred Liturgy said that this "full, conscious, and active participation" must be the aim considered before all else (14). This principle, however, should be understood in light of the whole document, which begins with a rather amazing statement: "This sacred council has set out to impart an ever-increasing vigor to the Christian lives of the faithful; to adapt more closely to the needs of our age those institutions which are subject to change; to encourage whatever can promote the union of all who believe in Christ; to strengthen whatever serves to call all of humanity into the Church's fold. Accordingly it sees particularly cogent reasons for undertaking the reform and promotion of the liturgy" (SC 1). This liturgy document was the first statement promulgated by the council, because the council fathers saw that renewing the Church had to begin with renewing the faithful through the liturgy. The ultimate goal is not a renewed liturgy. The liturgy must lead to renewed people who will then work to renew the earth. That's what Jesus came to do, and it's what he meant when he told us to "do this in memory of" him.

The dismissal really raises a fundamental question about the purpose of the Church. Many people, both in the past and in our own time, see the Church as primarily an institution whose job is to maintain the status quo. Religion is used to "bless" the established order and to resist calls for change in society. Religion was used, for example, to justify the continuation of slavery, and once that failed, to sustain discrimination and segregation. Religious leaders are called upon to bless military forces and to support wars against the "infidels" and the "godless" enemies of our country. Many people go to church with the assumption that they already live the way God wants them to live and they already know what God opposes and supports in society. So they expect the liturgy, and especially the preacher, to support what they already think and feel. Such an approach to religion does not leave much room for prophets or rabble-rousers or disturbers of the peace, even if it claims to follow Jesus who was all of those.

The liturgy, on the other hand, assumes that the Church exists for mission and that this mission is the same one that Jesus embraced at his baptism. The liturgy aims to promote the kingdom of God, which is a way of speaking about the difference between the way we live now and the way God wills for all people to live. The liturgy intends to change us so that we can cause change in our society. The change that happens in us is usually slow. That's one reason we need to come to worship week after week, year after year, so that the grace of God can continue to transform us. The mission we are given will not be accomplished quickly either. We come back to the liturgy Sunday after Sunday because we need to be strengthened again at the Table of the Word and the Table of the Bread in order to be able to continue the work of Christ for another week. We are to be agents of change, not defenders of the status quo.

This does not mean that the liturgy embraces any particular political or social solution to the world's problems. Preachers should address specific issues, lest they remain in the realm of pure abstraction, but only rarely will the proper response be clear. The liturgy seeks, rather, to shape us into people who will ask the right questions and embrace the right values so that we can seek solutions that are in accord with the Gospel. Father Robert Hovda described the kind of believers the liturgy seeks to form:

> A Christian should be distinguished by the fact that he sees the other person as deeply, fatherly-related brother or sister. It is not commitment to human solidarity alone, but to incomparable brotherhood that is the genius of faith.…A Christian should be distinguished by the fact that he pursues the goals of equity and peace as mandates, purposes of the living God. It is not commitment to political and economic revolution alone, but to creation's thrust toward unity and reconciliation that is the genius of faith. A Christian should be distinguished by the fact that he reverences sun and earth and air and water, all things, all beauty, as faint images of one who cares. It is not love of nature alone, but a feeling of kinship with and care for all the universe of things among which we claim a mastery and a responsibility that is the genius of faith.
>
> LIVING WORSHIP, JUNE 1970, VOL. 6, NO. 6

Hovda often spoke of the liturgy as a time for "playing kingdom" (See *Living Worship,* Nov. 1974, Vol. 10, No. 9). It is a time when we practice what life in the kingdom is like. In the liturgy we treat one another as deeply related brothers and sisters. We treat one another as equals and live in peace with all who are there. We seek reconciliation to overcome whatever divisions keep us apart. We bless God for water and oil and bread and wine and all the gifts of creation as we experience God's grace through them.

Some people, recognizing the gap between what we say and do in the liturgy and how we live when we are not at worship, criticize the liturgy for being irrelevant and out of touch with the reality of life. Some complain, for example, that they don't want to share a sign of peace at Mass with people they would not talk to outside of Mass. Perhaps the real question is why they would not talk to people outside of Mass with whom they have just shared the Body and Blood of the Lord. It may not be the liturgy that is out of touch, but perhaps our daily lives are too far removed from God's ways. We "play kingdom" to remind ourselves of God's values and how God wants us to live so that when we leave the liturgy we might move a bit closer to "kingdom living" during the week.

The core of that kingdom living, of course, is the core of Christ's message. We are to love God above all things and love our neighbor as ourselves. The liturgy calls us to practice both types of love during worship. We are not allowed to separate worship of God from our relationships with those around us, any more than we can separate love of God from love of our neighbor. Our worship is in vain if it does not lead us to imitate Christ in doing God's will and loving one another.

Pope John Paul II put it forcefully in his letter inaugurating the Year of the Eucharist in 2004: "We cannot delude ourselves: by our mutual love and, in particular, by our concern for those in need we will be recognized as true followers of Christ (cf. *Jn* 13:35; *Mt* 25:31–46). This will be the criterion by which the authenticity of our Eucharistic celebrations is judged" (*Mane Nobiscum Domine*, 28).

JOE'S JOURNEY

When Joe first began his catechumenate formation, he saw it as the way to join the Church. He wanted to find meaning for his life and to learn how to get to heaven. While these goals remained, he soon began to see that joining the Church involved more than his own salvation. Those in the catechumenate were often invited to join members of the parish in various works of charity and other activities that proclaimed God's love to others, including those who did not yet follow Christ. As he came to understand more about baptism itself, he learned that the call to baptism was a call to carry on the work of Christ in the world today. His own journey of spiritual growth has come to include growth in his care for others, especially those in need. As he prepares for baptism, he is becoming increasingly aware of what a privilege it is to be called by God to do Christ's work, even if living up to that call seems like a big challenge, too.

MARY'S JOURNEY

Mary has long understood that being a Catholic involves caring for others. Even as a child, she participated in clothing collections for the poor. She has always been as generous as she could be in the various collections for the missions and for the poor that come around every year. Since Paul died, she has been volunteering in the parish food pantry, and she has seen first-hand how people recognize God's love for them when the parish gives them a helping hand. What is new for Mary, though, is the close connection between these activities of charity and the sacraments. She has heard the pastor preach often about how her baptism commits her to service, and she is gradually coming to think of herself as called by God to carry on Christ's mission. When the priest dismisses the assembly at the end of Mass, she notices that sometimes he tells them to go in peace "to love and serve the Lord," and she counts on the strength she gains from the Eucharist to help her to do just that.

QUESTIONS FOR REFLECTION AND DISCUSSION

1. *Do you think of yourself as a missionary? Are you aware of being sent on mission at the end of every liturgy?*

2. *Do the announcements in your community help you see the connection between worship and the rest of the week? Can you give some examples? If they do not, what could be done to make that connection clearer?*

3. *What connections between your experience of worship and your daily living of the Gospel can you describe? Does the liturgy help you live the Gospel more fully?*

4. *What is the connection between liturgy and work for justice and peace?*

5. *What do you think is the primary purpose of the Church? What should it reinforce and what should it challenge?*

6. *Can you explain what Father Hovda meant when he called liturgy a time for "playing kingdom"? Does that describe your own experience of worship?*

7. *In light of Pope John Paul's criterion, how would you judge the authenticity of worship in your community of faith?*

RESOURCES FOR FURTHER READING

Franklin, R. W. and Robert L. Spaeth. *Virgil Michel: American Catholic*. Collegeville, MN: The Liturgical Press, 1988.

How Firm a Foundation: Voices of the Early Liturgical Movement. Kathleen Hughes, ed. Chicago: Liturgy Training Publications, 1990.

Liturgy and Justice. Koester, Anne, ed. Collegeville, MN: The Liturgical Press, 2002.

Living No Longer for Ourselves. Francis, Mark R. and Kathleen Hughes, eds. Collegeville, MN: The Liturgical Press, 1991.

Pecklers, Keith F. *The Unread Vision: The Liturgical Movement in the United States of America: 1926–1955*. Collegeville, MN: The Liturgical Press, 1998.

CHAPTER 12
Liturgy of the Hours

As the dismissal reminds us that our liturgical experience must extend throughout the week, so the Liturgy of the Hours can be understood as an extension of our worship throughout the hours of every day.

The *Catechism of the Catholic Church* says that the Liturgy of the Hours is "like an extension of the Eucharistic celebration" (1178). It keeps us aware of God throughout the day and offers praise to God at various times through the day.

The structure of the Liturgy of the Hours is a bit different than the liturgy of the various sacraments. It does not have a central ritual action like the meal of the Eucharist or the water bath of baptism. Its purpose is not to celebrate one particular moment or action, but to consecrate the unfolding hours of each day to God.

The shape of the Liturgy of the Hours is complex, partly because it derives from two different historical bases. These have been commonly called the cathedral office and the monastic office.

The cathedral office consisted primarily of two prayer

services, one at dawn and one at sunset. These morning and evening prayers were intended for the whole people of God, inviting them all to gather for prayer at the start and end of the day. The design of these prayer services was geared toward the larger community of the faithful. They included ritual actions and often used the same psalms and canticles each day so that the people learned to sing them easily.

The cathedral office also came to be called the canonical office because it was maintained at the cathedral in each city by a group of ministers called canons. They made sure that the prayer was offered, even when the faithful did not come together to pray. When any of the canons was traveling, he was expected to pray the office at the same time as his confreres at the cathedral. From this developed the requirement that the clergy recite the office daily, whether in common or alone.

The monastic office developed in monasteries where the monks met many times during the day and night for prayer. In addition to Morning and Evening Prayer, the monastic office included prayer at the third, sixth, and ninth hours of the day, night prayer called Compline, and prayer at midnight. It had been customary for all Christians to pray privately or in groups at all of those times except midnight. The monks developed that custom into communal liturgical prayer throughout the day.

The divine office, or breviary, that priests were required to pray in recent centuries was modeled largely on the monastic office. It included most of the monastic hours and used the whole psalter over a period of days or weeks. It came to be seen as simply the obligation of the clergy and of little interest to the laity. It was not uncommon, however, for parishes to celebrate Evening Prayer (Vespers) on Sundays, even into the twentieth century.

The Second Vatican Council called for a reform of the divine office with special emphasis on Morning and Evening Prayer as the "hinges on which the daily office turns." The council encouraged pastors to see to it that these "hours, especially Vespers, are celebrated in common in church on Sundays and on the more solemn feasts" (*SC* 100). The revision of the office issued after the council, however, was not really designed for parish use. It retains much of its character as a monastic discipline.

Some parishes, nevertheless, have reintroduced Morning and Evening Prayer as part of parish life. Sometimes Morning Prayer is celebrated instead of a weekday Mass, especially when a priest is not available for Mass. Evening Prayer is sometimes prayed before parish meetings or for the parish at large during Advent and Lent. Most efforts of this type draw on the cathedral office tradition as a model.

Both Morning and Evening Prayer have a similar structure, consisting of a hymn, psalms, a reading, a canticle, and intercessory prayer. The hymn and psalms are chosen to reflect the time of day and the focus of each liturgy, though they might also reflect the feast or season being celebrated.

Morning Prayer has the character of a dedication of the day to God. It sees the dawn of a new day as a symbol of resurrection and new life, as well as looking forward to the dawn of eternity. A theme of praise of God marks the office, which traditionally used the laudate psalms (Psalms 148–150) as a central element. Another psalm often used in Morning Prayer was Psalm 63, "O God, you are my God, I seek you...." A reading from Scripture is followed by the *Benedictus*, the canticle Zechariah sang at the birth of John the Baptist. Incense is sometimes burned in connection with the canticle. Then intercessions with a focus on the needs of the coming day are offered and concluded with the Lord's Prayer. A collect prayer and dismissal bring Morning Prayer to a close.

Evening Prayer has two traditional themes: thanksgiving for the gifts of the day and repentance for sins committed. Evening Prayer is similar in structure to Morning Prayer, though it may begin with a ritual lighting of lamps or candles, called the *lucenarium*. This practical action took on symbolic significance and became rather standard in the cathedral office. The hymn often spoke of evening, and Psalm 141 was often used because it speaks of an evening sacrifice: "Let my prayer be counted as incense before you, and the lifting up of my hands as an evening sacrifice." This verse also led to using incense with this psalm, though the Roman tradition used incense with the canticle of Mary (*Magnificat*) that comes after the reading. Like Morning Prayer, Evening

Prayer concludes with intercessions, the Lord's Prayer, a collect, and dismissal.

Jesus taught us to "pray always" (see Luke 18:1), and the Liturgy of the Hours is one way that the Church tries to fulfill that command. Those who share in this official prayer of the Church join themselves with the whole Church around the world. This prayer is the prayer of Christ himself, for we always pray as members of Christ's body; we offer our prayer in and through Christ. The *General Instruction of the Liturgy of the Hours* quotes St. Augustine:

> God could give us no greater gift than to establish as our Head the Word through whom he created all things and to unite us to that Head as members. The results are many. The Head is Son of God and Son of Man, one as God with the Father and one as man with us. When we speak in prayer to the Father, we do not separate the Son from him and when the Son's Body prays it does not separate itself from its Head. It is the one Savior of his Body, the Lord Christ Jesus, who prays for us and in us and who is prayed to by us. He prays for us as our priest, in us as our Head; he is prayed to by us as our God. Recognize therefore our own voice in him and his voice in us.

> *ENARRAT.* IN PSALM 85, 1
> QUOTED IN *GENERAL INSTRUCTION*
> *OF THE LITURGY OF THE HOURS*, 7

The General Instruction of the Liturgy of the Hours also offers this challenging vision:

> Lay groups gathering for prayer, apostolic work, or any other reason are encouraged to fulfill the Church's duty by celebrating part of the liturgy of the hours. The laity must learn above all how in the liturgy they are adoring God the Father in spirit and in truth; they should bear in mind that through public worship and prayer they reach all humanity and can contribute significantly to the salvation of the whole world.
>
> Finally, it is of great advantage for the family, the domestic sanctuary of the Church, not only to pray together to God but also to celebrate some parts of the liturgy of the hours as occasion offers, in order to enter more deeply into the life of the Church.
>
> *GENERAL INSTRUCTION*
> *OF THE LITURGY OF THE HOURS, 27*

That vision obviously has not yet come to life for most members of the Church. What the future holds remains to be seen.

JOE'S JOURNEY

In the course of his catechumenate experience, Joe has been introduced to a variety of forms of prayer. The team has taught them how to say the rosary, how to pray the

Stations of the Cross, and how to do centering prayer, along with various prayers they have memorized. Often they begin their catechetical sessions with a short form of Evening Prayer. Over time, the members of the group have come to value this prayer and its use of the psalms. Joe especially likes the idea of praying to God with the very words of Scripture, using language that Jesus himself must have used in his own prayer.

MARY'S JOURNEY

Mary has only experienced the Liturgy of the Hours on a few special occasions. The parish celebrates Evening Prayer on the Sundays of Advent and Lent as well as on major feasts that occur throughout the year. Mary used to think of these prayers as something just for priests and religious, but these parish celebrations have been both beautiful and prayerful. Mary has a couple of friends who tell her that they have been using the Liturgy of the Hours for their daily prayer, too. Mary hasn't adopted that practice yet, but she's thinking about it.

QUESTIONS FOR REFLECTION AND DISCUSSION

1. *Have you ever shared in any celebration of the Liturgy of the Hours? Did you find it prayerful? What do you remember most about it?*

2. *Does your community gather for Morning or Evening Prayer on any regular basis? If not, could you see a way to encourage that custom?*

3. *What are the main differences between the cathedral and monastic forms of the Liturgy of the Hours?*

4. *What is the focus of Morning Prayer? What are the main themes of Evening Prayer?*

5. *Could the Liturgy of the Hours be a useful part of your personal prayer life? Could it work as family prayer in your home?*

RESOURCES FOR FURTHER READING

General Instruction of the Liturgy of the Hours, Liturgy Documentary Series 5, Washington, D.C.: USCC Publications Office, 1983.

Martimort, Aimé Georges; Irénée Henri Dalmais, Pierre Jounel. *The Church at Prayer: Volume IV: The Liturgy and Time.* Collegeville, MN: The Liturgical Press, 1986.

Mayer, Laurence. *Morning and Evening Prayer in the Parish.* Chicago: Liturgy Training Publications, 1985.

Roguet, A.M. *The Liturgy of the Hours: The General Instruction With Commentary.* Collegeville, Minnesota: Liturgical Abbey Press. 1971.

Taft, Robert. *The Liturgy of the Hours in East and West: The Origins of the Divine Office and Its Meaning for Today.* Collegeville, MN: The Liturgical Press, 1986, 1993.

The Liturgy of the Hours: Study Text VII, The Bishops' Committee on the Liturgy. Washington, D.C.: USCC Publications Office, 1981.

CONCLUSION
Why Bother?

This book was written as an aid to those who take part in Christian worship, to help them enter more fully into the experience and to benefit more richly from it. But there is a deeper question that may be on the minds of some readers: why bother with liturgy at all? Why should we take the time to gather with other believers to worship God?

There are various ways to answer such questions. A basic response is simply that it is good for human beings to acknowledge the existence of God and their relationship to God. Doing so helps us to remember who we really are and where we fit in the grand scheme of the universe. That might keep us from the kind of arrogance that has led humans to rape the earth and oppress the poor. It can also keep us aware of how gifted we are and how gratefully we should live.

For believers in Christ, the liturgy offers needed support for living the Gospel way of life. Christianity is fundamentally a communal religion. We are not called by God as separate individuals but are called into a community of faith. We need to gather with one another on a regular basis to both offer and find support as we carry on the mission Christ entrusted to us. Gathering at least weekly to celebrate the Eucharist offers us regular contact with the Word of God to nourish and challenge our embrace of the Gospel values Jesus taught. It also feeds us with the Bread of Life and the Cup of Salvation, the meal that unites us intensely both with Christ and with one another. Nourished from both the Table of the Word and the Table of the Bread, we are strengthened to go out into the world to live the Gospel for another week.

Gathering for worship reminds us that we form the body of Christ in the world today. It reaffirms our bonds with all the other members of the body. It can provide the sense of community and belonging that every human needs to be fully alive. As Genesis teaches, it is not good for us to be alone. We are made for relationships, and we grow to completeness only in community with other people. Remembering how intimately our lives are entwined with others helps us to keep a healthy perspective on ourselves and those with whom we interact all week.

Many people today seem hungry for a deeper spirituality, for meaning in their lives. They seek it in all kinds of spiritual practices from various religions and philosophical traditions. Many openly say that they are interested in spirituality but not in religion. Yet the purpose of religion is to foster our spiritual lives, to bring us into union with God.

The liturgy is a powerful tool to foster that growth.

If we understand what we are doing and enter into it wholeheartedly, we will certainly find that it draws us deeper into ourselves and closer to God. We join with other believers to enact the rituals, and in doing so we act as the body of Christ assembled in union with our head. We worship the Father in and through Christ and thus are drawn into the mysterious workings of God in our world, as God gradually draws the whole universe toward unity with the God who is the source and center of all that is.

The richness of the liturgy has nourished countless believers through thousands of years. One who seeks to live life deeply and not just on the surface can find no better tutor than the liturgy of the Church.

Make a joyful noise to the Lord, all the earth.
  Worship the Lord with gladness;
  come into his presence with singing.
Know that the Lord is God.
  It is he that made us, and we are his;
  we are his people, and the sheep of his pasture.
Enter his gates with thanksgiving,
  and his courts with praise.
  Give thanks to him, bless his name.
For the Lord is good;
  his steadfast love endures for ever,
  and his faithfulness to all generations.

PSALM 100:1–5

Acknowledgments

Built of Living Stones: Art, Architecture, and Worship. Washington, DC: National Conference of Catholic Bishops/United States Catholic Conference, 2000.

Excerpt from Andy Griffith, *What It Was, Was Football* (pts. 1 & 2) single record (Capitol #2693), circa 1953.

Excerpts from Constitution on the Sacred Liturgy (*Sacrosanctum Concilium*), *Vatican Council II: The Basic Sixteen Documents,* edited by Austin Flannery, O.P., copyright © 1996, Costello Publishing Company, Northport, NY, are used by permission of the publisher. All rights reserved.

Excerpts from the English translation of the *Catechism of the Catholic Church for the United States of America,* copyright © 1994, United States Catholic Conference, Inc.—Libreria Editrice Vaticana. Used with permission.

Excerpts from the English translation of the *General Instruction of The Liturgy of the Hours* © 1974, International Committee on English in the Liturgy, Inc. (ICEL); excerpts from the English translation of *The Roman Missal* © 1973, ICEL; excerpts from the English translation of the *General Norms for the Liturgical Year and Calendar from Documents on the Liturgy, 1963-1979: Conciliar, Papal, and Curial Texts* © 1982, ICEL; excerpts from the English translation of *The General Instruction of the Roman Missal* © 2002, ICEL; excerpts from the English translation of *Order of Mass* © 2008, ICEL. All rights reserved.

Lebow, Victor. "Price Competition in 1955," p. 5, *Journal of Retailing,* Vol. XXXI, No. 1, Spring 1955.

Merton, Thomas. *The Living Bread* (New York: Farrar, Straus and Giroux, 1980). Copyright © 1956 by The Abbey of Our Lady of Gethsemani. All rights reserved.

Michel, Virgil. "The Scope of the Liturgical Movement," *Orate Fratres* 10 (1936), p. 485.

Pope John Paul II. *Dies Domini* (Apostolic letter on Keeping the Lord's Day Holy), May 31, 1998. Copyright © 1998 Libreria Editrice Vaticana.

———. *Ecclesia De Eucharistia* (Encyclical letter on the Eucharist In Its Relationship to the Church), April 17, 2003. Copyright © 2003 Libreria Editrice Vaticana.

———. *Mane Nobiscum Domine* (Apostolic Letter for the Year of the Eucharist), October 7, 2004. Copyright © 2004 Libreria Editrice Vaticana.

Pope Pius XII, *Mediator Dei* (Encyclical on the Sacred Liturgy), Nov. 20, 1947.

Other Titles on the Eucharist from Liguori Publications

WE WORSHIP
A Guide to the Catholic Mass

In his characteristic warm and down-to-earth manner, Father Oscar Lukefahr presents an uplifting and affirmative look at the Mass and its significance. *We Worship: A Guide to the Catholic Mass* explains the reason for worshiping at Mass, the different parts of the Mass, and the relevance of the Mass in our lives. The reader will learn how to "experience" the Mass, not just "watch it going by." This up-to-date book includes the revisions mandated in the new *General Instruction of the Roman Missal*, as well as a chapter devoted to frequently asked questions about the Mass.

ISBN 978-0-7648-1212-5

THE EUCHARIST
From Liguori's *50 Questions from the Pews* series

Designed to bring a better understanding of the Eucharist and the rituals involved in Mass, devotion, and prayer, this book is formatted in a way that is easy to read and understand. As it shows how prayer and worship form the core of the spiritual renewal of the Catholic community, this book addresses these questions and more: Is there a relationship between the altar and the Eucharist? What is the difference between the Sacred Heart of Jesus and the Eucharistic Heart of Jesus? What is Benediction? Religious and devotional practices are the language we use to communicate with God. *50 Questions from the Pews: The Eucharist* helps the reader participate more fully and richly in the Eucharist.

Condensed version also available (Spanish only)
20 Preguntas del Pueblo: LA EUCARISTÍA
ISBN 978-0-7648-1761-8

For prices and ordering information, call us toll free at
800-325-9521 or visit our Web site, www.liguori.org.